A RICH BOY'S GUIDE TO INVESTING

How Everyday People Can Achieve

Extraordinary Wealth and Leave Legacies

Wisdom Kwati

Ordering Details

To place orders or for details of discounts for bulk purchases by organizations or groups either for support, gift, training packages, fundraising, or any other educational purposes, send an email to wisdomkwati@gmail.com. Visit www.wisdomkwati.com or follow me on @Wisdom Kwati across all social media platforms.

Table of Contents

Chapter 1

INVESTING; THE PATH TO EXTRAORDINARY WEALTH

There is this young man who had never known the struggles that most people faced. He attended prestigious schools, wore designer clothes, and lived in a sprawling mansion. Yet, despite his opulent lifestyle, Oliver yearned for something more. He desired to make his own mark in the world, to create extraordinary wealth, not just inherit it.

One sunny afternoon, as Oliver strolled through the city streets, he noticed an intriguing figure. A man with a cloak and a wide-brimmed hat stood near a park bench, observing the passersby. Something about him seemed otherworldly, as if he possessed a wealth of knowledge beyond the ordinary.

Curiosity piqued, Oliver approached the mysterious stranger. "Excuse me, sir," Oliver said politely, "May I ask who you are?"

The man turned, a knowing smile playing on his lips. "Ah, Oliver Blackwood. The name carries great weight in these parts. I am known as Alexander Hartwood. Some call me a guide to extraordinary wealth."

Oliver's eyes widened. How did this man know his name? "Tell me more," Oliver urged, intrigued by the stranger's claim. Alexander gestured for Oliver to sit on the bench. "Oliver, my young friend, true wealth is not merely inherited, but created. It requires knowledge, strategy and a keen eye for opportunity. I can teach you how to turn ordinary investments into extraordinary wealth."

Oliver's interest was piqued. "But how can I, an everyday person, achieve such remarkable success? I have no experience in investing."

Alexander chuckled softly. "Ah, that is where the adventure begins, my young protégé. I shall be your guide, leading you through the labyrinth of investment opportunities, teaching you the secrets of the trade, and helping you navigate the treacherous waters of finance."

In the days that followed, Oliver met Alexander every evening in the library of his mansion. Alexander revealed a treasure trove of knowledge, sharing his expertise on stocks, bonds, real estate and various investment vehicles. Oliver soaked up the information like a sponge, his hunger for knowledge growing with each passing day.

Oliver discovered the power of diversification, learning how spreading investments across different industries could mitigate risk. He delved into the art of fundamental analysis, understanding how to evaluate a company's financial health and growth potential. Alexander introduced him to technical analysis, teaching Oliver how to read charts and identify patterns in stock prices.

As Oliver's knowledge grew, he began to make his first tentative steps into the world of investing. He purchased stocks, diligently following the advice of Alexander and conducting his own research. He watched the market with a hawk's eye, observing its ebbs and flows, learning to separate emotion from reason.

In today's world, wealth is often seen as a symbol of success and abundance. It provides individuals with the means to live a comfortable and fulfilling life, pursue their passions, and make a positive impact on the world. While there are various paths to wealth, one of the most powerful and proven methods is investing.

Investing is a way for people to make their money grow over time and open up opportunities for great financial success. It's like planting a seed that can grow into a big tree. In this chapter, we will talk about the idea of wealth, learn about the mindset of successful investors, understand the power of investing, and introduce the idea of investing in real estate for potentially big profits.

Wealth is not just about having a lot of money. It's about accumulating valuable things and having an abundance of resources. It includes more than just money and can include things like property, businesses, intellectual property (like inventions or creative works), personal relationships, good health, and overall well-being.

Having wealth is important because it can bring many benefits to our lives. Financial wealth provides security and freedom. It allows us to meet our needs, pursue our dreams and live a better life. It also gives us opportunities to grow as individuals, learn new things, and have experiences that can make our lives more fulfilling. Wealth also gives us the power to make a positive impact on our communities and support causes that are important to us.

The Mindset of Successful Investors

Have you ever looked at successful investors and wondered how they do what they do? Here is a secret -- their mindset. The mindset of successful investors plays a crucial role in their ability to create and sustain wealth. These individuals often possess key characteristics and habits that set them apart.

They have long-term vision. They always think ahead. Successful investors have a long-term perspective. They understand that wealth creation is a journey that requires patience, discipline and the ability to weather market fluctuations.

They have also mastered risk management. Investing involves risk and successful investors focus on managing and mitigating risks through diversification, thorough research and informed decision-making. They are not afraid of taking action, however, they take calculated actions.

These people are sold out to continuous learning. The investment landscape is constantly evolving. Successful investors are committed to ongoing education and staying updated on market trends, economic indicators and investment strategies. They seek out opportunities to expand their knowledge and skills.

They have built emotional discipline. It is no news that emotions can cloud one's judgment and lead to irrational investment decisions. Successful investors cultivate emotional discipline, remaining calm and objective in the face of market volatility. They make decisions based on thorough analysis and a solid investment thesis.

If there is anything I know that successful investors have, it is persistence and resilience. Building wealth through investing requires perseverance. Successful investors understand that setbacks and failures are part of the journey. They learn from their mistakes, adapt their strategies and remain resilient in the face of challenges.

Investing is a Means to Create Wealth

Investing is a powerful tool that can help you create wealth and achieve your financial goals. When you put money into various financial instruments or assets, there is this expectation of generating a return or profit over time. Of course, you know that investing comes with risks, but then, it also offers the potential for significant rewards and long-term growth.

Here are some key points to understand the power of investing as a means to create wealth:

Building wealth through compounding: When you invest your money, you have the opportunity to take advantage of a powerful concept called compounding, which can help you build wealth over time.

Compounding works like a snowball rolling down a hill. Initially, you invest a certain amount of money. Over time, that money has the potential to earn returns or profits. Instead of taking those returns out, you reinvest them along with your initial investment. As a result, your investment grows not only on the original amount but also on the accumulated earnings.

Here's an example to help illustrate how compounding works:

Let's say you invest $1,000 in an investment that has an average annual return of 8%. In the first year, your investment would grow by $80 (8% of $1,000), resulting in a total of $1,080. In the second year, the 8% return would apply to the increased amount, so your investment would grow by $86.40 (8% of $1,080), bringing the total to

$1,166.40. As time goes on, your investment continues to grow, and the returns generated become larger in value.

The real power of compounding comes into play when you allow your investments to grow over a long period. The longer you keep your money invested, the more time it has to compound and multiply.

For example, if you continue to invest $1,000 each year with an average annual return of 8% over 30 years, your investment can grow substantially. By the end of those 30 years, your initial investment of $1,000 each year would have turned into a much larger amount due to the compounding effect.

The key to maximizing the benefits of compounding is to start investing early and consistently, allowing your money more time to grow. This is why many financial advisors emphasize the importance of starting to invest as soon as possible.

Diversification and risk management: When you invest, you have the opportunity to spread your money across different types of investments, industries and parts of the world. This is called diversification.

Imagine you have a box of chocolates. If you put all your chocolates in one basket and accidentally drop it, you'll lose all your chocolates. But if you divide your chocolates into several smaller baskets and one of them falls, you'll still have chocolates in the other baskets. Diversification in investing works in a similar way.

When you invest in different types of assets, like stocks, bonds, real estate, and more, you spread your money across various baskets. Additionally, you can invest in different industries (e.g., technology, healthcare, finance) and different geographical regions (e.g., United States, Europe, Asia). This way, if one investment doesn't do well, the others may perform better and help balance things out.

Diversification is important because it helps manage risk. All investments come with some level of risk. If you put all your money into a single investment and it doesn't go as planned, you could lose a significant portion of your money. But if you have a diversified portfolio, the poor performance of one investment won't have as big of an impact on your overall portfolio. The other investments can help offset any losses.

The goal is to find a balance between potentially earning higher returns and minimizing risk. Diversification allows you to achieve this balance. It's like having a safety net for your investments. It doesn't guarantee profits or protect you from all losses, but it can help reduce the impact of poor performance on your overall investment.

Multiple investment options: Investing is a way of using your money to potentially make more money over time. It offers you various choices or "investment options" that you can pick from based on your personal preferences, financial goals and how much risk you're comfortable with.

These investment options include different types of things you can invest in, like stocks (which represent ownership in a company), bonds (which are like loans to companies or governments), real estate (such as properties or land), mutual funds (pools of money invested in various assets), exchange-traded funds (similar to mutual funds but traded on stock exchanges), commodities (like gold, oil or crops), and many more.

Each of these options has its own unique characteristics and potential for making money. Some investments may offer higher returns, but they can also be riskier. Others may be more stable but offer lower returns. When you understand the features of each investment option, you can create a "portfolio" that suits your preferences and objectives.

A portfolio is a collection of different investments that you own. For example, if you have a higher appetite for risk and want to potentially earn higher returns, you might choose to invest more in stocks. On the other hand, if you're more conservative and prioritize stability, you might prefer investing in bonds or real estate.

The idea is to diversify your investments, which means spreading your money across different types of assets. This helps reduce the overall risk because if one investment doesn't perform well, the others may still provide positive returns. It's like not putting all your eggs in one basket.

Long-term wealth creation: Investing is something you do for the long haul. The real magic of investing happens when you stay invested for a long time and let your money grow over the years. It's like planting a seed and watching it grow into a big tree.

The reason long-term investing works is because, historically, the stock market and other types of investments have shown an overall upward trend over many years, despite occasional drops along the way. This means that, over time, the value of your investments can increase.

Think of it like this: imagine you have a bumpy road with lots of ups and downs. But if you look at the road from a distance, you'll see that it gradually goes up. Investing is similar. In the short term, the value of your investments may go up and down due to market fluctuations, just like the bumps in the road. However, if you look at the bigger picture over a longer period, you'll notice that the overall trajectory is upward.

When you maintain a long-term perspective and stay invested, you give your money the chance to benefit from the growth of the economy and the power of compounding.

Beat inflation and preserve purchasing power: Inflation is the gradual increase in the prices of goods and services over time. When inflation occurs, the purchasing power of your money decreases because you can buy less with the same amount of money. For example, what you can buy for $10 today may cost $12 or more in the future due to inflation.

Investing can help you combat the effects of inflation. Instead of simply keeping your money in a savings account where it may not grow much, investing allows your money to potentially increase in value over time.

When you invest, you have the opportunity to choose assets that can generate returns, such as stocks, bonds or real estate. These investments have the potential to earn you more money than what you would earn from simply saving in a bank account. If your investment returns are higher than the inflation rate, you have a better chance of preserving and even growing your purchasing power.

Here's an example: Let's say the inflation rate is 2% per year. If you keep your money in a savings account that earns a 1% interest rate, your money is not keeping up with inflation. Your purchasing power is gradually decreasing because the rate of inflation is higher than the interest you're earning.

However, if you invest in assets that can potentially earn, let's say, a 5% return per year, you are outpacing the inflation rate. This means your investments have the potential to grow faster than the rate at which prices are increasing. By doing so, you have a better chance of preserving your purchasing power and potentially even growing it over time.

Long-term investments, especially those that have historically shown growth over time, like stocks or real estate, have the potential to outpace inflation and protect your wealth against its erosive effects. When you invest wisely, you increase the likelihood that your money will keep up with or even exceed the rising cost of living, helping you maintain your financial stability and purchasing power in the long run.

Financial independence and future goals: Investing plays a crucial role in achieving financial independence and reaching your long-term goals. It helps you accumulate the money you need to fulfill various aspirations in the future.

Think about your financial independence as the ability to support yourself and maintain your desired lifestyle without relying on others. It could mean having enough money to retire comfortably, fund your children's education, buy a home, start a business, or achieve any other significant goal you have in mind.

Investing provides you with a way to grow your money over time. By consistently setting aside a portion of your income and investing it wisely, you have the opportunity to harness the power of compounding.

Compounding is like a snowball effect. When you invest, your money has the potential to earn returns. Over time, these returns can generate additional returns. It's like a cycle of growth. The longer you stay invested, the more your money can grow through compounding.

When you compound your income, you increase the likelihood of accumulating the necessary funds to achieve your long-term goals. For example, if you consistently invest for retirement, your money can grow significantly over several years or decades. This growth can help you build a retirement nest egg that allows you to retire comfortably and enjoy financial independence.

Similarly, investing can help you save and grow money for other goals, such as funding your children's education, buying a home, or starting a business. By investing consistently and giving your money time to grow, you increase your chances of accumulating the funds needed to realize these aspirations.

The key is to start investing early and be consistent in your investment efforts. This way, you give your money more time to work for you and benefit from the potential growth of the investments you choose.

Investing provides you with the means to accumulate the necessary funds for financial independence and to reach your future goals. It allows your money to grow and work for you, bringing you closer to the life you envision for yourself and your loved ones.

However, it's important to note that investing involves risks. Markets can be volatile, and there are no guarantees of returns. It's crucial to conduct thorough research, understand your risk tolerance and diversify your investments appropriately. Seeking professional financial advice can also be valuable in navigating the complexities of investing.

Let's continue with Oliver's story.

Chapter 2

THE CONCEPT OF INVESTMENT

One day, as Oliver and Alexander walked through the bustling city streets, they stumbled upon a small, unassuming building. A sign read: "Blute Innovations - Where Dreams Become Reality." Intrigued, Oliver pushed open the door, and a world of technological marvels unfolded before him. The founder of Blute Innovations, Dr Emma Sinclair, greeted them warmly.

"Welcome, Oliver," Dr Sinclair said, her eyes twinkling with enthusiasm. "Here, we are at the forefront of innovation, creating products that change lives and disrupt industries. We invite you to invest in our vision."

Oliver's interest was immediately piqued. He listened intently as Dr Sinclair passionately described the groundbreaking projects underway at Blute Innovations. She spoke of revolutionary advancements in renewable energy, artificial intelligence and healthcare technology. The potential for extraordinary returns on investment seemed tangible, but Oliver's prudent nature urged him to exercise caution.

"I'm intrigued by your vision, Dr Sinclair," Oliver said, his brow furrowed with contemplation. "But before I invest, I would like to conduct my due diligence. Can you provide me with more information about the company's financials and growth projections?"

Dr Sinclair nodded appreciatively. "Of course, Oliver. We believe in transparency and are more than happy to share the necessary information. We have experienced significant growth over the past few years, with a strong track record of delivering innovative products to market. Our projections indicate exponential growth in the coming years, backed by a dedicated team of brilliant minds."

Impressed by Dr Sinclair's response, Oliver spent the following weeks meticulously analyzing the financial reports, studying market trends and conducting thorough research on the company's leadership and reputation. He also sought advice from Alexander, who provided invaluable guidance in assessing the potential risks and rewards of such an investment.

After careful consideration, Oliver made the decision to invest a portion of his wealth into Blute Innovations. It was a bold move, but he was confident in his due diligence and believed in the transformative power of the company's innovations.

To embark on a successful investing journey, it is essential to have a solid understanding of the basic concepts that underpin investment decisions. This chapter will explain key investment concepts such as risk and return, emphasize the importance of diversification, discuss different investment vehicles (stocks, bonds, and real estate), and identify their advantages and disadvantages.

Risk and Return

When we talk about risk and return in investing, it means that there is a trade-off between the potential for higher returns and the level of risk involved. Let's break it down:

Risk refers to the uncertainty or possibility of losing money on an investment. Whenever you invest your money, there is always some degree of risk involved. Different investments carry different levels of risk. For example, investing in stocks can be riskier because their prices can fluctuate a lot in the short term, while investing in government bonds may be considered less risky because they are backed by the government.

Return, on the other hand, represents the profit or gain that you can potentially earn from your investment. It is the money you make or the increase in the value of your investment over time. Generally, higher returns come with higher levels of risk. Investments that have the potential for higher returns often involve taking on more risk because there is a chance that you could lose some or all of your investment.

As an investor, it's important to assess the level of risk associated with an investment. This involves considering various factors such as how the market behaves, the overall economic conditions, any risks specific to the company or asset you're investing in, and the likelihood of achieving the desired returns. When you understand the risks involved, you can make more informed decisions about where to invest your money and how to manage your investment portfolio.

Importance of Diversification

Diversification is a risk management strategy that involves spreading investments across different asset classes, industries, sectors, and geographic regions. The goal of diversification is to reduce exposure to any single investment and minimize the impact of adverse events on the overall portfolio.

By diversifying, investors can potentially lower risk without sacrificing returns. Different asset classes tend to perform differently under varying market conditions. For example, stocks may perform well during periods of economic growth, while bonds may provide stability during market downturns. Diversification helps balance the portfolio and capture opportunities across various investments.

Investment Vehicles

Investment vehicles are different methods or options available for individuals to invest their money and potentially earn a return on their investment. Think of them as various types of vehicles that can help you reach your financial destination.

Just like there are different types of vehicles for transportation, such as cars, buses or trains, there are different investment vehicles to choose from when it comes to investing your money. Each investment vehicle has its own characteristics, benefits and risks. Some investment vehicles may be more suitable for certain goals or preferences.

Investment vehicles can include options like stocks, bonds, mutual funds, exchange-traded funds (ETFs), real estate, commodities, and more. Each of these investment vehicles operates in a unique way and offers different opportunities for growth and income.

Stocks: Stocks are like ownership shares in a company. When you buy stocks, you become a shareholder, which means you have a small piece of ownership in that company. By owning stocks, you have the potential to benefit from the company's profits and growth.

Investing in stocks requires ongoing research and analysis. It's important to stay informed about the companies you invest in, monitor their financial performance, and make decisions based on the information available.

Bonds: Bonds are like loans that governments, municipalities, and corporations take out to raise money. When you buy a bond, you're essentially lending your money to the issuer. In return, the issuer promises to pay you back the original amount you lent (known as the principal) when the bond matures. In the meantime, the issuer pays you periodic interest payments for the duration of the bond.

Real Estate: Real estate involves investing in properties such as residential, commercial or industrial buildings. Real estate investments offer the potential for rental income, capital appreciation, and tax advantages. Real estate can be a valuable investment vehicle for individuals looking to grow their wealth over time. It involves purchasing, owning, and managing properties with the goal of generating a financial return.

Mutual Funds: Mutual funds are investment vehicles that allow people to invest their money in a diversified portfolio without having to personally choose and buy individual stocks or bonds. Instead, investors buy shares of the mutual fund, and a professional manager is responsible for making investment decisions on behalf of all the fund's shareholders.

With mutual funds, you don't have to worry about researching and picking individual stocks or bonds. The fund manager, who is typically an experienced professional, takes care of this for you. They analyze the market, select investments, and make decisions to maximize returns.

Exchange-Traded Funds (ETFs): ETFs are investment funds that are similar to mutual funds in terms of providing diversification through a collection of securities. However, ETFs are traded on stock exchanges, just like individual stocks. This means that investors can buy and sell ETF shares throughout the trading day at market prices, whereas mutual funds are typically bought and sold at the end of the trading day at the net asset value (NAV) price.

Alternative Investments

Beyond traditional investment options like stocks, bonds, and real estate, there are alternative investment vehicles available to investors. These investments often have a low correlation with traditional assets and can provide diversification benefits.

Hedge Funds: Hedge funds are investment funds that are not available to everyone but are generally limited to wealthy or financially sophisticated individuals. The main goal of hedge funds is to generate profits for their investors using various investment strategies.

Private Equity: Private equity involves investing in privately-held companies or acquiring stakes in businesses that are not publicly traded. Private equity firms raise capital from institutional investors and high-net-worth individuals to invest in companies with growth potential. Private equity investments typically have a long-term investment horizon and can involve active management and operational improvements within the invested companies.

Venture Capital: Venture capital focuses on early-stage and high-growth companies with significant growth potential. Venture capital firms invest in these companies in exchange for an ownership stake. Investments in venture capital carry higher risks but also the potential for substantial returns if the invested companies succeed.

As an investor, it is important to conduct thorough research, consider their risk tolerance and investment goals, and seek professional advice when considering alternative investments. Understanding the basics of investing lays the foundation for making informed investment decisions.

Chapter 3

CAPITAL MARKET INVESTING

As the months passed, Oliver continued to refine his investment strategies under Alexander's watchful eye. He diversified his portfolio, allocating funds to different sectors and asset classes. He ventured into real estate, carefully selecting properties with growth potential. Oliver's confidence grew as his investments yielded positive results, gradually accumulating extraordinary wealth.

However, the journey was not without its challenges. Oliver encountered market downturns and economic fluctuations that tested his resolve. There were moments of doubt when fear and uncertainty gripped him. Yet, guided by Alexander's wisdom, Oliver learned to embrace volatility as an opportunity for growth.

Alexander imparted a crucial lesson: Successful investors are not swayed by short-term fluctuations but maintain a long-term perspective. They stay informed, adapt their strategies when necessary, and make decisions based on rational analysis rather than impulsive emotions. They master the market before they invest. Mastering the market will help you understand what each market entails and give you a heads up when investing.

Navigating the Capital Markets

Capital markets play a vital role in facilitating investment and capital allocation in the economy. They are platforms where individuals, businesses, and governments raise funds by issuing and trading financial securities. Some of the investment vehicles available within the capital markets include stocks, bonds, and mutual funds. These markets provide a mechanism for investors to buy and sell these investment instruments, enabling the flow of capital between investors and issuers.

Primary Market: In the primary market, new securities are issued and sold to investors. This is where companies and governments raise capital by selling stocks or issuing bonds for the first time through initial public offerings (IPOs) or bond offerings.

Secondary Market: The secondary market refers to the trading of previously issued securities among investors.

Stock exchanges and over-the-counter markets provide platforms for the buying and selling of stocks, bonds, and other financial instruments.

Factors Influencing the Performance of Capital Markets:

a. Economic Conditions: Capital markets are influenced by macroeconomic factors such as GDP growth, inflation rates, interest rates, and employment data. Positive economic indicators often lead to increased investor confidence and higher market performance, while negative economic indicators can have the opposite effect.

b. Market Sentiment: Investor sentiment and market psychology play a significant role in capital market performance. Optimistic sentiment can drive buying activity and push prices higher, while pessimistic sentiment can lead to selling pressure and market declines. Factors such as news events, geopolitical tensions, and investor confidence can influence market sentiment.

c. Corporate Earnings and Fundamentals: The financial performance of companies, including earnings reports, revenue growth, and profitability, can impact stock prices. Strong corporate fundamentals often lead to positive market performance, while weak financial results can result in price declines.

d. Monetary and Fiscal Policies: Central bank actions, such as interest rate changes and monetary policy decisions, can have a significant impact on capital markets. Similarly, government fiscal policies, including taxation, spending, and regulatory measures, can influence investor behavior and market performance.

e. Global Factors: Capital markets are interconnected, and global factors such as international trade, geopolitical events, and currency exchange rates can affect market performance. Economic developments in major economies around the world can impact investor sentiment and capital flows.

Investment Strategies for Capital Market Investments

While it is advised to invest in capital markets, you must also know the strategies that will help you get better returns as an investor. Some of them are:

a. Buy and Hold: The buy-and-hold strategy involves purchasing investments with a long-term perspective, intending to hold them for an extended period. This strategy takes advantage of long-term market trends and aims to benefit from capital appreciation and compounding over time.

b. Diversification: Diversification is the practice of spreading investments across different asset classes, sectors, and geographic regions to reduce risk. When you diversify, you can potentially mitigate the impact of your investment losses and enhance the overall risk-adjusted return of your portfolio.

c. Value Investing: Value investing involves identifying undervalued securities based on fundamental analysis. Here, you look for stocks or other assets that are trading at prices below their intrinsic value, with the expectation that their value will increase over time.

d. Growth Investing: Growth investing focuses on identifying companies or sectors with high growth potential. You seek out stocks or other assets of companies that are expected to experience above-average revenue and earnings growth. This strategy typically involves investing in industries or sectors that are poised for expansion.

e. Dollar-Cost Averaging: Dollar-cost averaging involves investing a fixed amount of money at regular intervals, regardless of market conditions. By consistently investing over time, you can mitigate the impact of short-term market volatility and potentially benefit from lower average purchase prices.

f. Risk Management: Implementing risk management strategies, such as setting appropriate asset allocation, diversifying investments, and using stop-loss orders, is crucial in capital market investing. Understanding personal risk tolerance and having a disciplined approach to risk management can help protect investments and minimize potential losses.

To succeed with capital market investing, you must stay informed, conduct thorough research, and align investment decisions with individual goals and risk tolerance. This way, you as an investor can navigate the capital markets with greater confidence and work towards achieving your financial objectives.

Chapter 4

REAL ESTATE INVESTING

Oliver's success did not go unnoticed by his peers. His transformation from a privileged young man to a self-made investor inspired many. Oliver realized that his journey was not solely about amassing wealth for himself but about empowering others to achieve financial independence and create their own extraordinary stories.

With Alexander's guidance, Oliver established the Blackwood Foundation, a philanthropic organization dedicated to financial literacy and empowerment. The foundation provided resources, workshops, and mentorship programs for individuals from all walks of life, empowering them to take control of their financial future.

Oliver's passion for sharing his knowledge led him to become a sought-after speaker at conferences and events, where he captivated audiences with his story and practical advice. He emphasized the importance of starting early, being disciplined, and continuously educating oneself in the ever-evolving world of investing.

Years turned into decades, and Oliver's extraordinary wealth continued to grow, not just in monetary terms, but in the impact he made on the lives of others. Through his investments, philanthropy, and commitment to financial education, Oliver's legacy transcended mere monetary gains. He became a beacon of hope for those who dared to dream, demonstrating that with knowledge, discipline, and a willingness to take calculated risks, anyone could create extraordinary wealth.

Real estate investing has long been recognized as a powerful wealth-building strategy. It is a popular and lucrative avenue for wealth creation. By investing in real estate, you can purchase, own, manage and sell properties with the goal of generating income and capital appreciation. Real estate on its own offers unique advantages that make it an attractive investment option for those seeking extraordinary returns. Here are some reasons you should consider Real Estate Investing:

Cash flow and passive income: When you invest in real estate, you can earn money in two main ways: through cash flow and passive income.

Cash flow is the money you receive regularly from your real estate investment. It comes from the rent paid by the people who are living or using your property. Let's say you buy a house or an apartment and rent it out to tenants. Every month, they pay you rent, and that becomes your cash flow. This money can be a steady and reliable source of income for you.

Passive income means that you don't have to actively work or put in a lot of effort to earn money from your real estate investment. Once you have set up the property and found good tenants, the rental income keeps coming in without requiring your constant involvement. It's like earning money while you sleep! This passive income can come from the rent you receive, and it can be used for different purposes.

You can use the rental income to cover your living expenses, such as paying your bills, buying groceries or even going on vacations. It can also be reinvested back into the real estate market to buy more properties and grow your investment portfolio. Another option is to use the money for diversification, which means spreading your investments across different types of assets or industries to reduce risk.

Appreciation potential: When we talk about the appreciation potential of real estate, we mean that over time, the value of the property can go up. While there may be ups and downs in the market from time to time, properties that are carefully chosen and located in desirable areas tend to increase in value over the long term.

Let's say you buy a house today for a certain amount of money. As the years go by, the value of that house may go up. This means that if you decide to sell the house in the future, you might be able to sell it for more than what you originally paid for it. This increase in value is called appreciation.

This appreciation can be a great way to accumulate wealth. If you hold onto the property for a while and its value increases, you can build up substantial wealth over time. This is particularly powerful when combined with the concept of compounding.

Leverage and control: When we talk about leverage and control in real estate investing, it means that you have the opportunity to use other people's money to finance your property purchases and have control over your investments.

Leverage in real estate refers to the ability to use borrowed money, such as a mortgage, to purchase a property. Let's say you want to buy a house, but you don't have all the money to pay for it upfront. In this case, you can take a mortgage loan from a bank or a lender. The loan allows you to use a portion of the bank's money to buy the property, while you contribute only a smaller portion of your own money as a down payment.

By using leverage, you can amplify your potential returns. If the value of the property increases over time, the return on your investment is based on the total value of the property, not just the amount of money you initially invested. This means that even though you only put in a portion of the purchase price, you can benefit from the full appreciation of the property.

Control in real estate investing means that as the owner of the property, you have the ability to make decisions and take actions that can increase its value. For example, you can make improvements to the property to make it more attractive or increase its rental rates. These improvements can add value to the property and potentially generate higher returns.

Having control over your real estate assets also means that you have the freedom to make decisions regarding the management of the property. You can choose the tenants, set the rental rates and make changes to the property to improve its income potential.

Tax benefits: When you invest in real estate, there are several tax advantages that can help you save money. These advantages come in the form of deductions, which means you can subtract certain expenses from your taxable income, potentially reducing the amount of taxes you owe. Here are some key tax benefits of real estate investing:

Property taxes: As a real estate investor, you are required to pay property taxes on the properties you own. The good news is that you can usually deduct these property taxes from your taxable income. Deducting property taxes helps lower the amount of income that is subject to taxes.

Mortgage interest: If you have a mortgage on your real estate investment property, a portion of your monthly mortgage payment goes towards paying the interest on the loan. The interest you pay on your mortgage can be deducted from your taxable income. This deduction can result in significant tax savings, especially during the early years of your mortgage when the interest portion of your payment is higher.

Maintenance costs: As a real estate investor, you incur various expenses to maintain and repair your investment property. These expenses can include things like fixing a leaky roof, replacing a water heater or repainting the property. The good news is that you can deduct these maintenance costs from your taxable income. Deducting these expenses helps offset your rental income and reduces the amount of taxes you owe.

Depreciation: Depreciation is a tax benefit that allows you to deduct the cost of your investment property over its useful life. The government recognises that properties tend to wear out and lose value over time. You can take advantage of this by deducting a portion of the property's value each year as a depreciation expense. This deduction can help offset your rental income and reduce your tax liability.

As a Nigerian, I understand that tax laws and regulations vary by country and jurisdiction. Therefore, you should consult with a tax professional or accountant who is familiar with the tax laws in your specific area to ensure you're maximizing the available tax benefits and following all applicable rules.

Portfolio diversification: Portfolio diversification means spreading your investments across different types of assets to reduce the overall risk of your investment portfolio. This will help you avoid putting all your eggs in one basket, so to speak.

Real estate investing is one way to achieve diversification. It involves investing in properties like houses, apartments or commercial buildings. These real estate assets have unique characteristics that can benefit your investment portfolio.

One advantage of real estate as an investment is that its value tends to behave differently compared to the stock market. When the stock market is doing well or poorly, real estate values may not necessarily move in the same direction. This is referred to as a low correlation. When two investments have a low correlation, their values don't tend to move together.

The benefit of this low correlation is that it helps reduce the overall volatility, or ups and downs, of your investment portfolio. In other words, if the stock market experiences a downturn, the real estate portion of your portfolio may not be affected in the same way. This can help protect your portfolio from severe losses during market downturns.

When you add real estate investments to your portfolio, you increase the diversity of your assets. This diversification can provide several advantages. First, it can potentially enhance your overall returns while managing risk. It is advisable to have different types of investments that don't move in lockstep, so you can earn a more stable return over time.

Second, if one investment performs poorly, the impact on your entire portfolio may be lessened. This is because the positive performance of other investments, such as real estate, can help offset the losses in another investment, like stocks. This way, the impact of any one investment's poor performance is reduced.

Hedge against inflation: Inflation means an increase in the prices of goods and services over time. When inflation occurs, the cost of living generally goes up, and the purchasing power of your money decreases. In other words, the same amount of money can buy you less than it could before.

Real estate, such as properties like houses or apartments, has historically been seen as a way to protect against the negative effects of inflation. Here's why:

Rental income: If you invest in real estate and rent out your property to tenants, you receive rental income. As the cost of living increases due to inflation, tenants may have to pay higher rents to cover their expenses. This means that your rental income can increase over time, providing a potential source of income that keeps pace with inflation. This can help you maintain the purchasing power of your money and mitigate the impact of rising prices.

Property values: Inflation can also have an impact on property values. As the cost of materials, labor and other factors involved in real estate development and construction increases, property values may rise as well. When you own real estate, such as a house or an apartment, the value of your property can appreciate over time. This means that if you decide to sell your property in the future, you may be able to sell it at a higher price due to inflation. This appreciation can serve as a safeguard against the erosion of purchasing power caused by rising prices.

We have seen why investing in real estate is the best choice to make today. However, it's important to note that real estate investing also comes with its own set of challenges and considerations. You must carefully analyze market conditions, conduct thorough due diligence on properties, manage tenants and property maintenance and navigate legal and regulatory requirements. Real estate investing requires a commitment of time, resources and expertise to maximize returns and mitigate risks.

Types of Real Estate Investments

    a. Residential Properties: Residential properties include single-family homes, duplexes, condominiums, townhouses, and apartment buildings. Investing in residential properties can provide a stable income stream through rental income. Residential properties are generally more accessible for individual investors starting in real estate investing.

b. Commercial Properties: Commercial properties include office buildings, retail spaces, warehouses, and industrial properties. Investing in commercial real estate offers the potential for higher rental yields and long-term lease agreements. However, commercial real estate often requires a larger capital investment and may involve more complex property management.

c. Rental Properties: Rental properties refer to properties specifically purchased for the purpose of generating rental income. This can include both residential and commercial properties. Rental properties can offer consistent cash flow, wealth accumulation through property appreciation, and tax advantages.

Strategies for Finding Profitable Real Estate Deals

a. Market Research: Conducting thorough market research is crucial in real estate investing. This involves analyzing supply and demand dynamics, economic indicators, population growth, job market conditions, and local amenities. Understanding the market trends and identifying areas with potential growth can lead to profitable investment opportunities.

b. Networking and Relationships: Building relationships with real estate professionals, such as real estate agents, brokers, and property managers, can provide access to off-market deals and valuable market insights. Networking with other investors and attending industry events can also lead to potential investment opportunities.

c. Due Diligence: Performing comprehensive due diligence is essential before investing in a property. This includes conducting property inspections, reviewing financial statements, analyzing rental income potential, assessing market rental rates, and evaluating the property's condition and potential for value-add opportunities.

d. Financing Options: Exploring different financing options is important in real estate investing. This can include traditional bank loans, private lenders, seller financing, or partnerships. Understanding the financing options available and securing favorable terms can enhance the profitability of real estate investments.

Potential Risks and Rewards of Real Estate Investing

Let's start with the rewards. Investing in Real Estate comes with a good number of rewards and they include:

Cash Flow: Real estate investments can provide a consistent income stream through rental income, allowing investors to generate passive cash flow.

Appreciation: Real estate has the potential for long-term appreciation, increasing the value of the investment over time.

Tax Advantages: Real estate investors can benefit from tax deductions, such as mortgage interest, property taxes, and depreciation, which can help reduce taxable income.

Leverage: Real estate investing allows for the use of leverage by using other people's money (such as mortgages) to finance the purchase of properties, potentially amplifying returns on investment.

Portfolio Diversification: Adding real estate to an investment portfolio can provide diversification, reducing overall portfolio risk by balancing exposure to different asset classes.

Now, aside from the rewards, there are also risks. These risks include:

Market Volatility: Real estate markets can experience fluctuations in property values due to economic conditions, supply and demand dynamics, and other factors. Market downturns can impact property prices and rental demand.

Financing Risks: Using leverage to finance real estate investments can increase risks, as mortgage payments and interest rates can affect cash flow and profitability.

Property Management: Owning and managing properties require time, effort, and expertise. Dealing with tenants, property maintenance, and repairs can be challenging and may require additional resources.

Vacancy and Cash Flow: Rental properties may experience periods of vacancy which can impact cash flow. Unanticipated expenses, such as repairs or property upgrades, can also affect profitability.

Regulatory and Legal Factors: Real estate investing is subject to various regulations and legal requirements. Understanding and complying with local laws, zoning regulations, and tenant rights is crucial to avoid legal issues.

It's important that you carefully assess these risks and rewards, conduct thorough research, and create a comprehensive investment strategy. Real estate investing requires a long-term perspective, due diligence, and the ability to adapt to market conditions.

Chapter 5

DEVELOPING A REAL ESTATE INVESTMENT STRATEGY

Oliver's journey from a rich boy yearning for purpose to a guiding light for others exemplified the transformative power of investing and the profound impact it could have on individuals and communities alike. His story became a testament to the idea that wealth was not solely measured by material possessions, but by the positive change one could bring to the world.

As Oliver approached the twilight years of his life, he reflected on the remarkable journey that had brought him to this point. He thought back to that fateful encounter with Alexander, the mysterious stranger who had opened his eyes to a world of opportunity and ignited his passion for investing. Without that chance meeting, Oliver realized he might have remained confined to the limited scope of his inherited wealth, never discovering his true potential.

Oliver's journey had been filled with highs and lows, successes and setbacks. But through it all, he had learned invaluable lessons that extended far beyond financial gains. He had learned the importance of humility, integrity, and gratitude. He had discovered the joy of giving back and the fulfillment that came from uplifting others.

He was able to build and sustain his wealth because aside from investing in real estate, he also created a blueprint that helped him in developing a real estate investment strategy.

Developing a solid real estate investment strategy is crucial for achieving success in the real estate market. One of them is your personal financial goals. Before diving into real estate investing, it is important to assess personal financial goals and align them with real estate investment objectives.

This involves considering factors such as desired return on investment, investment time horizon, risk tolerance, and available capital. Real estate investments should align with these goals, whether they involve generating passive income, long-term wealth accumulation, or portfolio diversification.

Assessing personal financial goals entails defining specific objectives, such as the desired level of cash flow, the timeline for achieving financial milestones, and the overall financial independence one seeks to attain. These goals will serve as a guiding framework for selecting appropriate investment strategies and properties.

After doing this, the next thing is to formulate a comprehensive investment plan tailored to individual circumstances. Formulating a comprehensive investment plan is a critical step in real estate investment. This plan should take into account your financial situation, risk tolerance and investment goals. Key components of the investment plan may include:

a. **Budgeting**: Determining the amount of capital available for investment, including down payments, financing options, and ongoing expenses (such as property management, maintenance, and insurance). It is essential to establish a budget that aligns with personal financial capabilities and objectives.

b. **Research and Education**: Investing time in research and education to understand the local real estate market, trends, and regulations. This includes analyzing market conditions, supply and demand dynamics, rental rates, and property values. Staying informed about the local market will help you identify potential investment opportunities and make informed decisions.

c. **Investment Criteria**: Defining specific investment criteria is crucial in the real estate investment plan. This involves considering factors such as property type (residential, commercial, multi-family), location preferences, target rental yield, and potential for appreciation. The investment criteria will help in narrowing down the options and focusing on properties that meet the desired objectives.

d. **Risk Management:** Developing risk management strategies is vital in real estate investment. This includes setting appropriate financial reserves, diversifying the investment portfolio across different properties or locations, and implementing contingency plans for unexpected expenses or changes in market conditions. Proper risk management minimizes potential losses and protects the investment.

e. **Exit Strategies:** Considering exit strategies for each investment property is essential. This involves planning for situations such as selling the property, refinancing, or converting it into a rental property. Having multiple exit strategies provides flexibility and ensures that the investment remains adaptable to changing market conditions.

Evaluating Different Real Estate Investment Strategies

To make better returns from your real estate investment, you need to have these strategies at the back of your mind:

a. Buy-and-Hold Strategy: The buy-and-hold strategy involves acquiring properties with the intention of holding them for an extended period, typically years or decades. The primary focus is on generating rental income and benefiting from property appreciation over time. Buy-and-hold investors often seek stable, cash-flowing properties in desirable locations with potential for long-term growth.

b. Fix-and-Flip Strategy: The fix-and-flip strategy involves purchasing distressed properties, renovating or improving them, and then selling them quickly for a profit. Fix-and-flip investors typically look for properties with significant upside potential and the ability to add value through renovations or repairs. This strategy requires a strong understanding of market dynamics, renovation costs, and the ability to accurately assess the potential profit margin.

c. Rental Properties: Investing in rental properties involves purchasing properties with the goal of generating consistent rental income. Rental property investors focus on cash flow and long-term wealth accumulation through property appreciation. This strategy involves selecting properties in locations with high rental demand and positive rental yield potential. Factors to consider include vacancy rates, rental market trends, tenant profiles, property management options, and iuimmmmmmmlllllllllllllllpotential rental income. Rental properties provide a steady income stream and the potential for long-term wealth accumulation.

Factors to Consider When Selecting Investment Properties

a. Location: Location is one of the most critical factors to consider when selecting investment properties. Properties in desirable locations tend to attract tenants, experience high demand, and have better potential for appreciation. Factors to consider include proximity to amenities, schools, transportation, job centers, and future development plans. A strong location can contribute to higher rental income and increased property value over time.

b. Property Condition: Assessing the condition of the property is essential to determine any potential repair or renovation costs. A thorough property inspection can help identify any underlying issues that may impact the investment. Consider the age of the property, structural integrity, maintenance requirements, and any necessary repairs or upgrades. Understanding the condition of the property ensures that the investment aligns with the desired level of effort and investment required.

c. Market Analysis: Conducting a comprehensive market analysis is crucial to evaluate the potential of an investment property. Analyze supply and demand dynamics in the local area, including vacancy rates, rental rates, and property values. Consider both current market conditions and future growth prospects. Understanding the local market trends and dynamics helps identify areas with strong investment potential.

d. Financial Analysis: Perform a detailed financial analysis to assess the potential returns and risks of the investment property. Consider factors such as purchase price, financing costs, rental income, operating expenses (property taxes, insurance, maintenance, property management fees), and projected cash flow. Evaluate the property's return on investment (ROI), cash-on-cash return, and other key financial metrics to ensure the investment aligns with your financial goals.

e. Rental Market Analysis: Analyze the rental market in the area to assess rental demand and potential rental income. Research local rental rates, vacancy rates, and tenant profiles. Understanding the rental market dynamics helps determine the feasibility of generating positive cash flow and the potential for rental income growth over time.

f. Legal and Regulatory Considerations: Understand the legal and regulatory considerations specific to the investment property. Research zoning regulations, landlord-tenant laws, and any specific requirements or restrictions that may impact the property's use or rental operations. Compliance with local laws and regulations is essential to protect the investment and avoid legal issues.

g. Property Management: Consider the management requirements of the investment property. Determine whether you will manage the property yourself or hire a professional property management company. Evaluate the costs associated with property management and the impact on your time and resources. Property management can ensure smooth operations, tenant screening, rent collection, maintenance, and minimize potential issues.

Evaluating these key factors helps you as an investor select properties that align with your investment goals, risk tolerance, and financial capabilities. Thorough due diligence, research, and consultation with real estate professionals can significantly enhance the chances of success in real estate investing.

Chapter 6

FINANCING YOUR INVESTMENTS

Oliver's success and the impact of his investments began to catch the attention of prominent individuals in the financial industry. One such person was Elizabeth Reynolds, a renowned venture capitalist known for her keen eye for emerging technologies and startups.

Elizabeth reached out to Oliver, expressing admiration for his investment prowess and the positive changes he had brought about through the Blackwood Foundation. She proposed a partnership that would combine Oliver's financial acumen and Elizabeth's expertise in identifying disruptive technologies and promising startups.

Intrigued by the potential of this collaboration, Oliver agreed to join forces with Elizabeth. Together, they established the Blackwood-Reynolds Investment Fund, a venture capital fund dedicated to supporting innovative startups with high growth potential.

Oliver and Elizabeth carefully curated a portfolio of investments, focusing on industries such as clean energy, biotechnology, artificial intelligence, and sustainable agriculture. They sought out entrepreneurs who shared their vision of creating positive change in the world while generating extraordinary returns for investors.

As the Blackwood-Reynolds Investment Fund flourished, Oliver and Elizabeth saw firsthand the transformative power of capital allocation. The startups they supported not only achieved financial success but also made substantial contributions to society. Clean energy companies revolutionized the way we generated and consumed power, biotech firms developed life-saving medications, and sustainable agriculture initiatives addressed global food security challenges.

When it comes to real estate investing, understanding the basics of mortgages and exploring different financing options is crucial. In this chapter, we will delve into the fundamentals of mortgages, the various financing options available for real estate investments and the insights on how to secure favorable financing terms.

A mortgage is a loan provided by a financial institution to finance the purchase of a property. The borrower (property buyer) pledges the property as collateral for the loan, and the lender (usually a bank or mortgage company) provides the funds based on the property's value and the borrower's financial qualifications.

Imagine you want to buy a car, but you don't have enough money to pay for it upfront. So, you decide to get a car loan from a bank. A mortgage is similar, but instead of buying a car, you're buying a house.

Key aspects of mortgages include:

Loan Amount: This is the amount borrowed, which is typically a percentage of the property's purchase price or appraised value. The loan amount is like the total cost of the car. When you get a mortgage, it represents the total amount of money you're borrowing from the bank to buy the house. It's usually a percentage of the house's price or its appraised value, which is an estimate of how much the house is worth.

Interest Rate: This is the cost of borrowing, expressed as an annual percentage, which determines the amount of interest paid over the loan term. The interest rate is like the interest you pay on your car loan. It's a cost you have to pay for borrowing the money. The interest rate for a mortgage is expressed as an annual percentage and determines how much extra you'll need to repay on top of the loan amount.

Loan Term: This is the length of time over which the loan is repaid, typically ranging from 15 to 30 years. The loan term is like the duration of your car loan. It's the length of time you have to repay the mortgage. Just like car loans can be paid off in a few years, mortgages typically have terms that range from 15 to 30 years.

Down Payment: This is the initial upfront payment made by the borrower, expressed as a percentage of the property's purchase price. The down payment is like the upfront payment you make when buying a car. It's the initial amount you pay from your own savings to reduce the loan amount. The down payment for a house is usually expressed as a percentage of the house's price.

Amortization: This is the repayment schedule that outlines how the loan principal and interest are paid over the loan term. Amortization is like the payment schedule for your car loan. It outlines how you'll repay the loan over time. With a mortgage, it shows how much of your monthly payment goes towards paying off the loan principal (the actual borrowed amount) and how much goes towards paying interest.

Monthly Payments: This is the regular payments made by the borrower to repay the loan, which typically include principal, interest, property taxes, and insurance (referred to as PITI). The monthly payments for a mortgage are similar to the monthly payments you make for your car loan. They include the principal (the amount you borrowed), interest (the cost of borrowing), and other expenses like property taxes and insurance. These payments are made regularly until the mortgage is fully paid off.

So, you can say that a mortgage is a loan you get from a bank to buy a house. It involves borrowing a specific amount of money, paying interest on that amount, making regular monthly payments, and repaying the loan over a set period of time.

Financing Options Available for Real Estate Investments

Imagine you want to start a business, but you don't have enough money to fund it yourself. So, you explore different options to borrow money from various sources. Financing options for real estate investments work in a similar way, where you borrow money to invest in a property.

a. Traditional Mortgages: Traditional mortgages are the most common form of financing for real estate investments. They typically require a down payment (ranging from 3% to 20% of the property's purchase price) and have fixed or adjustable interest rates. Traditional mortgages are offered by banks, credit unions, and mortgage lenders.

   Traditional mortgages are like getting a loan from a bank to start your business. They are the most common form of financing for real estate investments. You typically need to make a down payment (an upfront payment) when you buy the property, and then you make regular payments over time to repay the loan. Traditional mortgages can have fixed or adjustable interest rates, just like business loans can have fixed or variable interest rates.

b. Government-Backed Loans: Government-backed loans, such as FHA (Federal Housing

Administration) loans and VA (Veterans Affairs) loans, are options available for eligible borrowers. These loans offer more flexible qualification requirements and lower down payment options.

They are like special loan programs specifically designed for certain types of entrepreneurs. FHA loans are popular among first-time business owners, while VA loans are available to eligible veterans and active-duty military personnel. These loans often have more flexible qualification requirements and lower down payment options compared to traditional mortgages.

c. Portfolio Loans: Portfolio loans are offered by some banks or credit unions and are not sold to investors on the secondary mortgage market. These loans provide more flexibility in terms of eligibility requirements and can be suitable for borrowers with unique financial situations or properties that don't meet conventional loan criteria.

Portfolio loans are like customized loans that you might get from a private investor for your business. Some banks or credit unions offer these loans and keep them within their own portfolio instead of selling them to other investors. This gives them more flexibility in terms of eligibility requirements, making them suitable for borrowers with unique financial situations or properties that don't meet the standard loan criteria.

d. Hard Money Loans: Hard money loans are short-term, asset-based loans typically used by real estate investors for fix-and-flip projects. These loans are secured by the property and are based on the property's value rather than the borrower's creditworthiness. Hard money loans have higher interest rates and shorter repayment terms.

Hard money loans are like short-term, high-interest loans that entrepreneurs sometimes use for specific business projects. In the real estate world, they are commonly used by investors for fix-and-flip projects. These loans are secured by the property itself, rather than being based solely on the borrower's creditworthiness. Just like in business, hard money loans have higher interest rates and shorter repayment terms compared to other financing options.

e. Private Financing: Private financing involves obtaining loans from individuals or private investors. These loans are negotiated directly between the borrower and the lender, allowing for more flexible terms and potentially faster approval processes.

Private financing is like borrowing money from individuals or private investors who believe in your business idea. In real estate, you can negotiate directly with these lenders for loans. This allows for more flexible terms, such as repayment schedules and interest rates, and potentially faster approval processes compared to traditional lenders.

So, you can go with traditional mortgages from banks, government-backed loans designed for specific groups, customized portfolio loans from certain lenders, short-term hard money loans for specific projects, or seek private financing from individuals or private investors. Each option has its own advantages and considerations, depending on your needs and qualifications.

How to Secure Favorable Financing Terms

Securing favorable financing terms means obtaining a loan or financial agreement with the most beneficial conditions for the borrower. It's like getting a loan with terms that work in your favor, making it easier and more affordable to borrow money for a specific purpose, such as buying a house or investing in real estate.

To secure favorable financing terms for real estate investments, consider the following strategies:

Build a Strong Credit Profile: Maintain a good credit score by paying bills on time, managing existing debt responsibly, and keeping credit utilization low. A higher credit score increases the likelihood of securing favorable interest rates and loan terms.

Save for a Larger Down Payment: A larger down payment reduces the loan amount and can lead to more favorable loan terms. Saving for a significant down payment demonstrates financial stability and lowers the lender's perceived risk.

Shop Around for Lenders: Different lenders may offer varying interest rates, loan terms, and fees. It's advisable to research and compare multiple lenders to find the most competitive financing options for your investment.

Improve Debt-to-Income Ratio: Lenders evaluate the borrower's debt-to-income ratio to assess their ability to repay the loan. Lowering existing debt and increasing income can improve this ratio, increasing the chances of obtaining favorable financing terms.

Prepare a Strong Loan Application: Present a comprehensive loan application that includes accurate financial information, property details, and a compelling investment plan. Providing detailed documentation and demonstrating a solid investment strategy can increase the lender's confidence in your application.

Consider Professional Assistance: Engaging a mortgage broker or real estate attorney can provide valuable guidance and help navigate the financing process. These professionals have expertise in securing favorable financing terms and can assist in negotiating loan terms on your behalf.

Understanding mortgages and exploring different financing options is crucial in real estate investing. With this, you can optimize your real estate investment endeavors and maximize your potential for success.

Chapter 7

NAVIGATING THE
REAL ESTATE MARKET

News of the Blackwood-Reynolds Investment Fund's successes spread throughout the financial industry, attracting the attention of international investors and influential figures. Oliver and Elizabeth found themselves invited to global conferences, where they shared their investment strategies and the importance of investing in ventures that made a positive impact on society.

Through their international engagements, Oliver and Elizabeth forged partnerships with like-minded investors, government entities, and philanthropic organizations. They established the Global Wealth Empowerment Initiative (GWEI), a collaborative effort aimed at promoting sustainable investing and empowering individuals worldwide to create extraordinary wealth for themselves and their communities.

WEI launched various programs, including financial literacy campaigns, entrepreneurship training, and impact investment accelerators. These initiatives provided individuals from all walks of life with the knowledge, skills, and resources to participate in the global economy, leveraging investments to drive social and environmental change.

Oliver and Elizabeth became vocal advocates for sustainable investing, appearing on television interviews, writing influential articles, and addressing audiences at prestigious forums. Their message resonated with people around the world, inspiring a new wave of socially responsible investors who sought to align their financial goals with their values.

As Oliver and Elizabeth approached retirement age, they contemplated the future of their mission. They recognized the need for a seamless transition, ensuring that their efforts would continue to impact generations to come.

With great care and consideration, Oliver and Elizabeth selected a new generation of leaders to oversee the Blackwood-Reynolds Investment Fund and the GWEI.

These individuals shared their vision, passion, and commitment to using wealth as a force for positive change.

Oliver and Elizabeth took on advisory roles, offering guidance and wisdom to the next generation. They remained active in philanthropic endeavors, focusing on initiatives related to education, healthcare, and environmental conservation.

Before making a decision, it's important to do your homework and gather all the necessary information. This process is called due diligence. Conducting thorough due diligence means taking the time to dig deep into the details of the property you're interested in. Here are a few key steps involved:

Research: Start by researching the property and the surrounding area. Look into factors like property values, recent sales in the neighborhood, and any development plans or infrastructure projects that might impact the property's value.

Property Inspection: Hire a professional inspector to thoroughly examine the property. They will check for any structural issues, potential repairs needed, or any other problems that may affect the property's condition and value.

Legal and Financial Review: Review important legal documents such as property titles, leases, contracts, and financial statements. It's important to understand any legal obligations or restrictions tied to the property and to assess its financial performance.

Environmental Assessment: Depending on the property type and location, it may be necessary to assess any potential environmental risks or concerns. This is particularly important if the property has a history of hazardous materials or is located in an environmentally sensitive area.

Market Analysis: Conduct a thorough market analysis to understand the demand and supply dynamics of the area. Look at factors like rental rates, vacancy rates, and comparable property sales to evaluate the property's potential income and future growth.

Other aspects of due diligence include:

Title Search: Review the property's title history to ensure there are no liens, encumbrances, or legal disputes that could affect the ownership or future saleability of the property. Some of the documents to look out for include:

1. Deed of Conveyances

2. Certificate of Occupancy (C of O)

3. Deed of Assignment

4. Survey Plan

5. Building Plan Approval

6. Excision

7. The Sale and Purchase Agreement

8. Governor's Consent

9. Deed of Mortgage

10. Grant of Probate

Financial Analysis: Perform a detailed financial analysis to evaluate the property's income potential, operating expenses, and return on investment. Consider factors such as rental income, vacancy rates, property taxes, insurance, maintenance costs, and property management fees.

Legal and Regulatory Compliance: Verify that the property complies with local zoning regulations, building codes, and any other legal requirements. Also, review any existing leases or rental agreements to understand the current tenant situation.

Environmental Assessment: Assess any potential environmental risks or liabilities associated with the property. This may involve conducting environmental site assessments or reviewing past environmental reports.

Market Comparison: Compare the property to similar properties in the area to assess its market value, rental rates, and potential for appreciation. Understanding the local market will help determine if the property is priced competitively and has the potential for positive cash flow.

Evaluating Market Conditions

Understanding market conditions is crucial when it comes to making informed decisions about investing in real estate. To put it simply, you need to know what's happening in the real estate market to make smart choices. Here are a few important factors to consider:

Supply: This refers to the availability of properties in the market. You'll want to assess how many properties are currently for sale or rent, as well as any new construction projects or upcoming developments that could affect the supply of properties. If there are many properties available, it might indicate more options for buyers or renters. On the other hand, limited supply could create higher demand and potentially increase property values.

Demand: This is all about how many people are looking to buy or rent properties in a specific market. It's important to evaluate factors like population growth, the job market, and demographic trends that can influence the demand for housing. If there is a growing population and a strong job market, it generally suggests a higher demand for housing.

Absorption Rate: The absorption rate measures how quickly properties are being sold or rented in a particular market. A high absorption rate indicates that properties are being sold or rented quickly, which suggests a strong demand. A low absorption rate, on the other hand, may indicate that there is an oversupply of properties in the market, which could potentially lead to longer selling or rental periods.

Rental Market: If you're interested in rental properties, it's important to analyze the rental market. This involves looking at vacancy rates (the percentage of rental units that are unoccupied), rental rates, and rental trends. Factors such as population growth, job opportunities, and the demand for rentals from specific demographics (like students, young professionals, or families) can impact the rental market.

By evaluating these factors, you can gain insights into the current and future potential of a real estate market. This information helps you make informed decisions about buying or renting properties. Keep in mind that market conditions can change over time, so it's important to stay updated and seek advice from real estate professionals who have expertise in the local market.

Economic Indicators in Real Estate Investments

Economic indicators provide valuable insights into the overall health and performance of the economy, and they can have an impact on real estate investments. Here are some key economic indicators to consider and how they can influence real estate investments:

GDP Growth: Gross Domestic Product (GDP) measures the total value of goods and services produced in a country or region. Analyzing the GDP growth rate helps assess the overall economic performance. When the economy is growing, it often leads to increased job opportunities, rising incomes, and higher demand for real estate. This can potentially drive property values and rental demand.

Interest Rates: Interest rates refer to the cost of borrowing money for mortgages and loans. Monitoring interest rate trends is important because it affects the affordability of financing for real estate purchases. Lower interest rates make borrowing more affordable, stimulating real estate activity and increasing demand. Conversely, higher interest rates can impact affordability and potentially reduce demand for real estate.

Employment Market: Evaluating the job market conditions is crucial. Factors such as unemployment rates, job growth, and industry trends provide insights into the strength of the job market. A robust job market attracts population growth and drives demand for housing. When there are more jobs and employment opportunities, it can have a positive impact on real estate investments.

Inflation: Inflation refers to the increase in the prices of goods and services over time. Monitoring inflation rates is important because it affects the purchasing power of consumers and the cost of living. Inflation can influence rental rates and property values. Real estate investments can act as a hedge against inflation because rental income and property values may increase alongside inflation.

Infrastructure and Development: Consider infrastructure projects and development plans in the area where you are considering investing. Improvements in transportation, public amenities, and commercial developments can have a positive impact on property values and rental demand. Upcoming infrastructure projects can indicate potential growth and increased demand for real estate in the area.

By monitoring these economic indicators, real estate investors can gain insights into the broader economic conditions and make more informed investment decisions. It's important to note that economic conditions can change over time, so staying updated and seeking advice from professionals can help navigate the real estate market effectively.

Market Analysis Tools and Techniques in Real Estate

Economic indicators provide valuable insights into the overall health and performance of the economy, and they can have an impact on real estate investments. Here are some key economic indicators to consider and how they can influence real estate investments:

GDP Growth: Gross Domestic Product (GDP) measures the total value of goods and services produced in a country or region. Analyzing the GDP growth rate helps assess the overall economic performance. When the economy is growing, it often leads to increased job opportunities, rising incomes, and higher demand for real estate. This can potentially drive property values and rental demand.

Interest Rates: Interest rates refer to the cost of borrowing money for mortgages and loans. Monitoring interest rate trends is important because it affects the affordability of financing for real estate purchases. Lower interest rates make borrowing more affordable, stimulating real estate activity and increasing demand. Conversely, higher interest rates can impact affordability and potentially reduce demand for real estate.

Employment Market: Evaluating the job market conditions is crucial. Factors such as unemployment rates, job growth, and industry trends provide insights into the strength of the job market. A robust job market attracts population growth and drives demand for housing. When there are more jobs and employment opportunities, it can have a positive impact on real estate investments.

Inflation: Inflation refers to the increase in the prices of goods and services over time. Monitoring inflation rates is important because it affects the purchasing power of consumers and the cost of living. Inflation can influence rental rates and property values. Real estate investments can act as a hedge against inflation because rental income and property values may increase alongside inflation.

Infrastructure and Development: Consider infrastructure projects and development plans in the area where you are considering investing. Improvements in transportation, public amenities, and commercial developments can have a positive impact on property values and rental demand. Upcoming infrastructure projects can indicate potential growth and increased demand for real estate in the area.

When you monitor these economic indicators, you as an investor can gain insights into the broader economic conditions and make more informed investment decisions. It's important to note that economic conditions can change over time, so staying updated and seeking advice from professionals can help navigate the real estate market effectively.

By conducting thorough due diligence, evaluating market conditions, analyzing economic indicators, and utilizing market analysis tools and techniques, you can make well-informed investment decisions in the real estate market. This proactive approach helps mitigate risks, identify opportunities, and maximize the potential for long-term success in real estate investing.

Chapter 8

MITIGATING RISKS IN REAL ESTATE INVESTMENT

Years later, as Oliver reflected on his journey, he marveled at the transformation that had occurred. What had started as a personal quest for purpose and wealth had evolved into a global movement, empowering individuals to create extraordinary wealth while making a lasting impact on the world.

Oliver's story, once that of a rich boy seeking meaning, had become a testament to the potential within each person to effect change. The journey had not only enriched his own life but had also touched countless others, opening doors of opportunity, and elevating communities.

As Oliver looked out at the world he had helped shape, he felt a deep sense of fulfillment. The impact of his investments and the collective efforts of the Blackwood-Reynolds Investment Fund and GWEI had created a ripple effect that extended far beyond what he had ever imagined.

Communities once plagued by poverty were now thriving with the establishment of local businesses, job opportunities, and improved access to education and healthcare. Innovations driven by sustainable investments had transformed industries, reducing carbon emissions, and mitigating the effects of climate change. The power of investing has brought about a more equitable and sustainable world.

Oliver's heart swelled with pride as he witnessed the accomplishments of those he had mentored and supported. Former scholarship recipients had become successful entrepreneurs, philanthropists, and advocates for change in their own right. They had embraced the teachings of financial literacy and responsible investing, paying it forward to uplift others and create a cycle of prosperity.

The legacy of Oliver Blackwood and Elizabeth Reynolds lived on, not just in the investment funds and philanthropic initiatives they had established, but in the hearts and minds of those they had touched. Their story had become a guiding light, inspiring a new generation of individuals to use their wealth, influence, and knowledge to create extraordinary wealth and leave a positive impact on the world. He was able to come this far because he mastered how to mitigate risks.

Real estate investing involves certain risks that investors need to be aware of and manage effectively. Here are some strategies for mitigating risks, understanding insurance options and coverage, implementing risk mitigation strategies, and addressing legal considerations and compliance:

Risks Associated with Real Estate Investing

Before making real estate investment decisions, it is important to identify and assess potential risks. Common risks in real estate investing include:

Market Risk: Fluctuations in property values and market conditions can impact investment returns. To mitigate this risk, conduct thorough market analysis, evaluate economic indicators, and stay informed about market trends.

Financing Risk: Dependence on financing exposes investors to risks such as interest rate fluctuations, loan defaults, and challenges in refinancing. To manage this risk, maintain healthy financial ratios, consider fixed-rate mortgages, and have contingency plans in case of financing difficulties.

Cash Flow Risk: Insufficient rental income or high vacancies can disrupt cash flow. Conduct proper due diligence on rental demand, market rental rates, and property management strategies to mitigate cash flow risk.

Property Risk: Physical damage, maintenance issues, and unexpected repairs can impact investment returns. To manage this risk, conduct property inspections, perform preventive maintenance, and have reserve funds set aside for property-related expenses.

Legal and Regulatory Risk: Failure to comply with local laws, regulations, and zoning restrictions can result in penalties, fines, or legal disputes. To mitigate this risk, engage legal professionals, understand local regulations, and ensure proper documentation and compliance.

Liability Risk: Accidents, injuries, or property damage can expose investors to legal liabilities. To manage this risk, obtain adequate liability insurance coverage, implement proper safety measures, and consider legal structures for asset protection.

Insurance Options and Coverage for Investment Properties

Insurance plays a crucial role in protecting real estate investments. Consider the following insurance options for investment properties:

Property Insurance: Property insurance covers damages to the physical structure, such as fire, vandalism, natural disasters, and theft. Ensure that the coverage amount is sufficient to rebuild or repair the property in case of damage.

Liability Insurance: Liability insurance protects against claims or lawsuits for injuries or property damage that occur on the investment property. It provides coverage for legal defense costs and potential settlements.

Rent Loss Insurance: Rent loss insurance compensates for lost rental income due to unforeseen circumstances like tenant default, property damage, or extended vacancies. It helps mitigate the impact of rental income disruptions.

Umbrella Insurance: Umbrella insurance provides additional liability coverage beyond the limits of primary property and liability insurance policies. It offers protection against substantial claims or lawsuits that exceed the underlying coverage.

Title Insurance: Title insurance protects against potential ownership disputes, liens, or other title-related issues. It provides coverage for losses resulting from defects in the property's title.

Consulting with insurance professionals specializing in real estate can help assess the specific insurance needs for investment properties and obtain appropriate coverage tailored to your investment goals and risks.

Risk Mitigation Strategies

Implementing risk mitigation strategies is crucial to protect real estate investments. Consider the following strategies:

Asset Protection: Establish legal structures such as limited liability companies (LLCs) or trusts to protect personal assets from potential risks associated with investment properties. This can help isolate liability and safeguard personal wealth. Think of asset protection as putting a protective shield around your personal assets, like a fortress protecting its treasures.

By establishing legal structures such as LLCs or trusts, you create a barrier that separates your personal assets (e.g., your home, savings) from potential risks associated with investment properties. This way, if something goes wrong with your investment, your personal assets are shielded from being affected.

Contingency Planning: Develop contingency plans to address unforeseen events that may impact the investment, such as property damage, rental income disruptions, or economic downturns. Maintain sufficient reserves to cover unexpected expenses and income shortfalls.

Contingency planning is like having a backup plan in case of unexpected events, similar to carrying an umbrella on a cloudy day. Just as an umbrella helps protect you from getting wet when it rains, developing contingency plans helps you prepare for unforeseen circumstances that can impact your investment, such as property damage, rental income disruptions, or economic downturns. By setting aside sufficient reserves, you have a safety net to cover unexpected expenses and income shortfalls, ensuring that your investment stays secure.

Diversification: Diversification is like having a varied menu of different dishes to choose from instead of relying on a single meal. In real estate, it means spreading your investments across different property types, locations, and investment strategies. By diversifying, you're not putting all your eggs in one basket.

Just as enjoying a variety of dishes reduces the risk of not liking one particular meal, diversifying your real estate portfolio helps spread risks. So, if one investment doesn't perform as well as expected, the others can help balance it out and protect your overall returns.

Professional Partnerships: Think of professional partnerships as assembling a reliable team to support you, much like a sports team working together towards a common goal. Engaging reputable property managers, contractors, and legal professionals who specialize in real estate is like having skilled teammates who handle various aspects of your investment. They ensure efficient property management, maintenance, and legal compliance, allowing you to focus on the bigger picture and reducing the risk of overlooking important details.

By implementing these risk mitigation strategies, you can protect your real estate investments, just as the analogies of fortresses, umbrellas, diverse menus, and sports teams help illustrate their importance in a more relatable way.

Legal Considerations and Compliance in Real Estate Investing

Legal considerations and compliance are important aspects of real estate investing. It means understanding and following the legal requirements and rules that govern real estate transactions. This helps protect your investment and ensures a smooth and problem-free process. Let's explore some key points:

Local Laws and Regulations: It's crucial to become familiar with the laws and regulations specific to the area where you're investing. These may include rules about zoning, building codes, renting properties, and paying taxes. By following these laws, you can avoid penalties, fines, or legal complications.

Contracts and Agreements: When buying or leasing properties, working with contractors, or entering into partnerships, it's important to use legally binding contracts and agreements. These documents clearly state the terms and conditions of the agreement and protect the interests of all parties involved. It's wise to consult with legal professionals to ensure the contracts are well-drafted and favorable to you.

Tenant Laws and Rights: If you plan to rent out properties, it's essential to understand the rights and obligations of tenants as defined by local tenancy laws. These laws cover areas such as lease agreements, security deposits, rent increases, eviction processes, and tenant privacy. Following these laws helps maintain a positive relationship with your tenants and reduces legal risks.

Fair Housing Laws: Fair housing laws prohibit discrimination based on race, color, religion, sex, national origin, disability, or familial status. It's important to comply with these laws and treat all prospective tenants fairly and equally during the screening and rental process. Familiarize yourself with the protected classes and ensure you don't engage in discriminatory practices.

Tax Obligations: Real estate investments come with tax obligations that you need to understand and fulfill. Consult with tax professionals to ensure compliance with local tax laws, including reporting rental income, paying property taxes, capital gains taxes, and taking advantage of any applicable deductions or exemptions.

Environmental Regulations: Environmental regulations are important considerations, particularly if the property has potential environmental liabilities. Understanding environmental assessments, remediation requirements, and compliance with environmental protection laws is essential to avoid legal issues and potential financial liabilities.

Disclosure Requirements: You have a legal obligation to disclose any known property defects or hazards, such as lead-based paint (if applicable) or other material information that may impact the value or desirability of the property. Complying with these disclosure requirements ensures transparency and protects both you and the buyer or tenant.

Intellectual Property Protection: If you have any intellectual property associated with your real estate investments, such as trademarks, logos, or proprietary information, it's important to protect those rights. Consult with legal professionals to establish appropriate measures to safeguard your intellectual property.

Ongoing Legal Monitoring: Real estate laws and regulations can change over time. It's important to stay updated on any changes that may affect your investments. Regularly review and monitor your legal obligations to ensure continued compliance and to avoid any legal pitfalls.

When you understand and adhere to these legal considerations and compliance requirements, you can protect your investments, avoid legal issues, and ensure a smooth and successful real estate investing journey.

Seeking guidance from legal professionals specializing in real estate law is highly recommended to ensure full compliance with applicable regulations and to address any specific legal concerns related to your investment strategy. Compliance with legal requirements not only protects your investments but also fosters trust and credibility in your real estate ventures.

Chapter 9

GROWING YOUR PORTFOLIO

Once you have successfully established your real estate investment strategy and gained experience in the market, you may want to consider scaling up your portfolio and diversifying your investments. Scaling refers to expanding your real estate holdings and increasing the number of properties you own. This chapter will discuss the strategies for scaling your real estate investments, diversifying through various asset classes, and optimizing returns while considering tax implications.

Financing Options: To scale your real estate investments, you can explore different financing options. These options may include traditional bank loans, private lenders, partnerships, or syndications. I shared more about these in my book, THE RULE ESTATE. When you access additional capital through these avenues, you can acquire more properties and grow your portfolio.

Equity Growth: As you own properties, they have the potential to appreciate in value over time. The rental income generated by your properties can also increase. When you reinvest the profits from your existing properties into new investments, you can use the equity (the value of your properties minus any outstanding loans) to fund the purchase of additional properties. This strategy allows you to leverage the growth of your existing investments to expand your portfolio.

Leveraging Relationships: Building strong relationships with lenders, real estate professionals, and fellow investors is important when scaling your real estate investments. These connections can provide valuable insights, access to deals, and potential partnerships. By leveraging these relationships, you can gain access to more opportunities and resources that support your efforts to scale your portfolio.

Systematize and Delegate: As your portfolio grows, it becomes essential to develop systems and processes to streamline property management. This involves creating efficient procedures for tasks such as rent collection, maintenance, and tenant management. Delegating these tasks to property managers or a professional team can free up your time and allow you to focus on acquiring and scaling your portfolio. By systematizing and delegating, you can ensure that your properties are well-managed while you focus on expanding your real estate holdings.

Scaling your real estate investments requires careful planning, financial considerations, and leveraging available resources. By implementing these strategies, you can effectively grow your portfolio and diversify your real estate holdings, ultimately maximizing your investment returns.

Diversifying Real Estate Asset Classes

Diversification is a key strategy for reducing risks and maximizing potential returns in real estate investing. It involves spreading your investments across different types of properties, known as asset classes. By diversifying, you can reduce the impact that any one property or sector can have on your overall investment performance. Let's explore some common asset classes in real estate:

Residential Properties: These are properties where people live, such as single-family homes, condominiums, townhouses, or buildings with multiple apartments.

Residential properties offer stable rental income and the potential for the property value to increase over time.

Commercial Properties: Commercial properties are used for business purposes and include retail spaces, office buildings, industrial warehouses, and mixed-use properties. Investing in commercial properties can provide higher rental yields and the possibility of securing long-term leases with businesses.

Industrial Properties: Industrial properties consist of warehouses, distribution centers, and manufacturing facilities. With the rise of e-commerce and the need for logistics infrastructure, investing in industrial properties can be lucrative, as they cater to the growing demand for storage and distribution spaces.

Hospitality Properties: Hospitality properties include hotels, resorts, and vacation rentals. Investing in this asset class allows you to generate income through room rates, occupancy rates, and tourism trends. However, it's important to consider the cyclical nature of the hospitality industry and the potential impact of economic downturns.

Specialized Properties: Specialized properties refer to niche sectors within real estate, such as healthcare facilities, student housing, self-storage units, or senior living facilities. These sectors can offer unique investment opportunities and potentially higher returns due to specific market demands and demographics.

When you diversify your real estate portfolio across these asset classes, you can spread the risks associated with any particular property type or sector. This means that if one sector experiences a downturn, the performance of other sectors may help offset potential losses. Diversification allows you to take advantage of different market conditions and increase your chances of achieving favorable investment returns.

Passive Investment Options

Passive real estate investment options provide an opportunity to diversify your investment portfolio without the responsibilities and time commitment of directly owning and managing properties. Here are some options to consider:

Real Estate Investment Trusts (REITs): REITs are like companies that own, operate, or finance income-generating real estate properties such as shopping malls, apartment buildings, or office spaces. By investing in REITs, you can become a shareholder and benefit from the rental income and profits generated by the properties owned by the REIT. It's similar to investing in stocks, but instead of buying shares of individual companies, you're investing in a portfolio of real estate properties.

Real Estate Crowdfunding: Crowdfunding platforms allow individuals to pool their money together to invest in real estate projects. These platforms provide access to a wide range of investment opportunities, such as residential developments, commercial properties, or even specific projects like a hotel renovation or a housing development. By contributing a smaller amount of money, you can become a part-owner of these projects and potentially earn returns based on the project's success.

Real Estate Syndications: Syndications involve pooling funds with other investors to acquire larger properties or participate in real estate development projects. In this case, experienced real estate professionals, called sponsors, manage the investment on behalf of the investors.

When you investing in a real estate syndication, you can benefit from the expertise and resources of these sponsors, who handle tasks like property acquisition, management, and deal structuring. This allows you to passively invest in larger properties or projects that may be beyond your individual investment capacity.

Passive real estate investment options offer several advantages. They provide convenience because you don't have to deal with the day-to-day management of properties. They also offer diversification, allowing you to spread your investment across different properties or projects.

Additionally, these options provide accessibility to the real estate market with smaller investment amounts compared to purchasing a property outright. However, it's important to carefully research and understand each investment option, including its potential risks, returns, and any associated fees, before making an investment decision.

Analyzing Tax Implications and Optimizing Returns

Understanding the tax implications of real estate investments is important for maximizing your returns. Here are some strategies to consider:

Depreciation Benefits: Depreciation is a tax benefit that allows you to deduct the cost of your investment property over its useful life. By properly depreciating your property, you can reduce your taxable income, which means you may owe less in taxes. It's a way to account for the wear and tear and decrease in value of the property over time.

1031 Exchange: A 1031 exchange, also known as a like-kind exchange, is a strategy that allows you to sell one investment property and buy another similar property without incurring immediate capital gains taxes. By using this exchange, you can defer the taxes on the profit you made from selling the first property and reinvest that money into a new property. This strategy can help you grow your real estate portfolio without losing a significant portion of your profits to taxes.

Tax-Advantaged Accounts: Explore options like self-directed individual retirement accounts (IRAs) or 401(k)s to invest in real estate. These accounts offer tax advantages, such as tax-deferred or tax-free growth, depending on the account type. By using these accounts, you can invest in real estate and potentially enjoy tax benefits that can help your investments grow more efficiently.

Capital Gains Strategies: Capital gains taxes are applied when you sell a property for a profit. Timing the sale strategically can help you optimize your tax liability.

Depending on how long you held the property, you may qualify for different tax rates. By understanding the implications of short-term (properties held for a year or less) and long-term (properties held for more than a year) capital gains, you can plan your property sales to minimize the taxes you owe.

Tax Deductions: Real estate investors can benefit from various tax deductions. These deductions include expenses such as mortgage interest, property taxes, repairs and maintenance, and depreciation. By properly documenting and claiming these deductions, you can reduce your taxable income, which ultimately lowers your tax bill.

Professional Tax Guidance: Real estate taxation can be complex, so it's a good idea to seek the assistance of qualified tax professionals who specialize in real estate investments. These professionals can help you navigate the tax landscape, identify applicable deductions and credits, and ensure compliance with tax laws. They have the expertise to optimize your tax situation and help you make informed decisions.

Remember, taxes can have a significant impact on your real estate investment returns. By understanding and implementing these strategies, you can potentially minimize your tax liabilities and optimize the returns on your investments. Always consult with qualified tax professionals to ensure you are making informed decisions based on your specific circumstances.

Optimizing returns also involves analyzing various factors beyond taxes, including rental income, property appreciation, and operating expenses. Regularly review and assess the performance of your investment properties, make informed decisions based on market conditions, and consider refinancing or selling underperforming assets to reallocate capital.

Chapter 10

NURTURING LONG-TERM SUCCESS

Once you have a real estate portfolio, it's important to manage it effectively to ensure long-term success. Managing your investment properties properly is crucial for maximizing returns and maintaining their value. Here are some strategies to consider:

Regular Maintenance: It's important to take care of your properties by implementing a proactive maintenance plan. This involves conducting regular inspections to identify any issues, addressing repairs promptly, and maintaining a preventive maintenance schedule. By staying on top of maintenance tasks, you can minimize potential problems and tenant complaints, keeping your properties in good condition.

Tenant Relations: Building positive relationships with your tenants is key. It involves being responsive to their communication and addressing their concerns promptly. Creating a safe and comfortable living environment is important as happy tenants are more likely to renew their leases and take good care of the property. Good tenant relations can lead to long-term, stable rental income.

Efficient Rent Collection: Establishing streamlined rent collection processes is important to ensure timely payments. By utilizing online rent payment systems, you can offer convenience to your tenants and automate the rent collection process. This reduces the risk of late or missed payments, helping you maintain consistent cash flow and avoid unnecessary complications.

Property Security: Protecting your investment properties is essential. This involves implementing appropriate security measures to prevent theft or vandalism. Installing secure locks, considering surveillance systems, and educating tenants on safety measures can help create a sense of security for both you and your tenants. A secure property reduces the risk of damage and ensures a safe environment for everyone involved.

Doing these will help maintain the value of your investment properties, attract reliable tenants, and maximize your returns. Effective management is key to long-term success in real estate investing.

Maximizing Rental Income and Minimizing Expenses

When it comes to real estate investments, maximizing rental income and minimizing expenses are important for increasing your cash flow and overall profitability. Here are some strategies to consider:

Rental Market Analysis: It's important to stay informed about rental market trends. By conducting regular market analysis, you can ensure that your rental rates are competitive while also maximizing your income potential. This means keeping an eye on what similar properties are charging for rent in your area and adjusting your rates accordingly.

Value-Add Improvements: Look for opportunities to add value to your rental properties. This could involve renovating units, upgrading amenities, or adding desirable features that allow you to charge higher rents and attract quality tenants. By enhancing the appeal and functionality of your properties, you can justify higher rental rates and potentially increase your rental income.

Expense Management: Take the time to review and optimize your property's operating expenses. This involves seeking competitive bids from vendors for maintenance and repairs, exploring energy-efficient upgrades to reduce utility costs, and renegotiating service contracts to minimize expenses. By finding ways to reduce your expenses without compromising on the quality of your property, you can improve your cash flow and overall profitability.

Lease Renewals: Encourage your tenants to renew their leases. By maintaining strong tenant relations, addressing their concerns promptly, and offering incentives for lease renewals, you can minimize turnover and vacancy periods. Tenant turnover can be costly due to the expenses associated with finding new tenants, preparing the property for new occupants, and potential loss of rental income during vacant periods. By focusing on lease renewals, you can stabilize your cash flow and reduce associated costs.

Monitoring and Evaluating Investment Performance

Monitoring and evaluating the performance of your real estate investments is essential for making informed decisions and identifying areas where you can improve. Here are some strategies to consider:

Financial Reporting: It's important to maintain accurate and up-to-date financial records for each property in your portfolio. This includes income statements, balance sheets, and cash flow statements. By regularly reviewing these financial reports, you can keep track of the financial health and performance of your investments. This information will help you understand how much money is coming in from rent, how much is going out in expenses, and whether your investments are generating positive cash flow.

Key Performance Indicators (KPIs): Establishing key performance indicators allows you to measure and track the performance of your properties. These KPIs can include metrics such as occupancy rates (how many units are rented out), rental growth (how much the rent is increasing over time), operating expenses as a percentage of income (how much you're spending on expenses relative to your rental income), and return on investment (ROI). By monitoring these indicators, you can gauge the success of your investments and identify areas for improvement.

Benchmarking: It's important to compare the performance of your properties against industry benchmarks and similar properties in the market. This analysis helps you understand how your properties are performing relative to others in terms of occupancy rates, rental income, expenses, and overall profitability. By benchmarking your properties, you can identify areas where you may be falling behind or excelling, allowing you to make adjustments to improve efficiency, increase revenue, or reduce costs.

Regular Evaluations: Conduct periodic evaluations of your properties to assess their condition, market positioning, and potential for value appreciation. This involves reviewing factors such as property condition, rental demand, competition, and overall performance. By evaluating each property in your portfolio, you can determine whether it aligns with your investment goals and make informed decisions about its future.

This way, you can stay informed about the performance of your real estate investments, identify areas for improvement, and make informed decisions to optimize your portfolio's performance.

Developing Exit Strategies and Realizing Investment Profits

When it comes to real estate investing, having a well-defined exit strategy is important for realizing profits and achieving your investment goals. Here are some strategies to consider:

Market Timing: It's important to stay informed about market conditions and consider timing your exit based on favorable trends. By monitoring factors like property values, rental demand, and interest rates, you can make informed decisions about when to sell your property for the best possible return on investment.

Property Disposition: Evaluate whether selling a property aligns with your investment objectives. Take into account factors such as property appreciation (how much the property has increased in value), current market conditions, projected cash flow, and your portfolio diversification goals. By carefully considering these factors, you can determine if selling a property will help you achieve your investment goals.

1031 Exchange: A 1031 exchange is a strategy that allows you to defer capital gains taxes when selling one investment property and using the proceeds to purchase another qualifying property. This strategy can be useful if you want to grow your real estate portfolio while delaying your tax obligations. It provides an opportunity to reinvest the proceeds into another property without immediately paying taxes on the capital gains.

Refinancing: Refinancing involves exploring options to access the equity (the increased value) in your properties. By refinancing, you can take advantage of the higher value of your properties and use the funds for further investments or other financial goals. Refinancing can be a way to access cash without selling the property.

Portfolio Optimization: Regularly review your real estate portfolio to identify underperforming properties or those that no longer align with your investment strategy. If certain properties are not generating the expected returns or no longer fit your investment goals, consider selling or exchanging them to optimize your portfolio composition and maximize your overall returns.

Estate Planning: It's important to incorporate estate planning considerations into your exit strategy. This involves determining how your real estate assets will be managed or transferred to heirs or beneficiaries, minimizing tax liabilities, and ensuring a smooth transition of ownership. Estate planning allows you to plan for the future and make sure your real estate investments are handled according to your wishes.

Remember, it's always a good idea to consult with professionals such as real estate agents, property managers, accountants, and financial advisors. They can provide guidance and assist you in formulating and executing effective exit strategies that align with your long-term investment objectives.

Chapter 11

BEYOND REAL ESTATE

While real estate can be a lucrative investment, diversifying your investment portfolio with non-real estate assets is essential for achieving a well-rounded and balanced approach to wealth creation. While real estate can be a valuable wealth-building channel, there are also other avenues to consider diversifying your investments and expanding your wealth. Here are a few examples:

Stock Market Investments

Stocks are like ownership shares in a company. When you buy stocks, you become a shareholder, which means you have a small piece of ownership in that company. By owning stocks, you have the potential to benefit from the company's profits and growth.

One advantage of owning stocks is the potential for capital appreciation. This means that if the company performs well and its value increases over time, the price of the stock can go up, allowing you to sell it at a higher price and make a profit.

Another advantage is the potential for dividend income. Some companies distribute a portion of their profits to shareholders as dividends. If you own stocks in a company that pays dividends, you can receive regular payments as a shareholder.

However, it's important to note that stocks also come with higher levels of volatility and risk compared to other investment options. The price of stocks can fluctuate a lot in the short term, which means their value can go up and down frequently. This volatility can make the value of your investment change quickly.

The advantages of stocks include the potential for high returns, meaning you have a chance to earn a lot of money if the company does well. Stocks are also relatively liquid, which means you can easily buy and sell them on the stock market.

Additionally, owning stocks allows you to participate in the success of well-performing companies. If a company you own stocks in grows and becomes more profitable, the value of your stocks may increase.

However, there are also disadvantages to investing in stocks. One is market volatility, which means that the value of stocks can fluctuate significantly, and you may experience losses if the market declines. There is also the risk of individual stock losses if a particular company you own stocks in performs poorly.

Investing in stocks requires ongoing research and analysis. It's important to stay informed about the companies you invest in, monitor their financial performance, and make decisions based on the information available.

Bonds and Fixed Income Investments

Bonds are debt instruments issued by governments, municipalities, and corporations. When you invest in bonds, you essentially lend money to the issuer in exchange for regular interest payments and the return of the principal amount at maturity. Bonds are generally considered lower-risk investments compared to stocks.

Bonds are like loans that governments, municipalities, and corporations take out to raise money. When you buy a bond, you're essentially lending your money to the issuer. In return, the issuer promises to pay you back the original amount you lent (known as the principal) when the bond matures. In the meantime, the issuer pays you periodic interest payments for the duration of the bond.

One advantage of bonds is that they provide a fixed income stream. This means that you can expect regular interest payments from the issuer at specific intervals, such as annually or semi-annually. This can be particularly attractive if you're looking for a stable and predictable source of income.

Compared to stocks, bonds generally have lower volatility. This means that the value of bonds tends to be less likely to fluctuate drastically in the short term. This lower volatility can provide a sense of stability in your investment portfolio.

Bonds also come with a relatively lower level of risk, although it depends on the creditworthiness of the issuer. If you're investing in bonds issued by a government or a highly reputable corporation, there is typically a lower risk of default. This means the likelihood of the issuer being unable to repay the principal or make interest payments is relatively low.

However, there are some disadvantages to investing in bonds as well. One is that the potential returns from bonds tend to be lower compared to other investment options like stocks. This is because bonds are generally considered safer investments, and lower risk usually translates to lower potential returns.

Another risk associated with bonds is interest rate risk. When interest rates rise, the prices of existing bonds can decline. This means that if you need to sell your bond before it matures, you might receive less money for it than what you initially paid. However, if you hold the bond until maturity, you will still receive the promised principal back.

Additionally, inflation can erode the purchasing power of fixed interest payments. If the rate of inflation is higher than the interest rate offered by the bond, the real value of your interest payments may decrease over time.

Mutual Funds and Exchange-Traded Funds (ETFs): Mutual funds and ETFs pool money from multiple investors to invest in a diversified portfolio of stocks, bonds, or other assets. They offer the benefit of professional management and diversification across different securities. Mutual funds are typically actively managed, while ETFs are passively managed and aim to track the performance of specific indexes.

Mutual Funds

Mutual funds are investment vehicles that allow people to invest their money in a diversified portfolio without having to personally choose and buy individual stocks or bonds. Instead, investors buy shares of the mutual fund, and a professional manager is responsible for making investment decisions on behalf of all the fund's shareholders.

With mutual funds, you don't have to worry about researching and picking individual stocks or bonds. The fund manager, who is typically an experienced professional, takes care of this for you. They analyze the market, select investments, and make decisions to maximize returns.

Mutual funds also pool money from multiple investors to invest in a wide variety of assets, such as stocks, bonds, or both. This diversification helps reduce the risk of losing all your money if one particular investment performs poorly. By spreading your money across different investments, you can potentially minimize the impact of any single investment's ups and downs.

It also offers investors the opportunity to invest in various types of assets, such as stocks, bonds, real estate, or commodities. This allows you to gain exposure to different sectors of the economy or different parts of the world, depending on the fund's focus.

On the other hand, bear in mind that mutual funds charge fees for their services, such as management fees and expense ratios. These fees can vary among funds and may be higher compared to other investment options. It's essential to understand the fees associated with a mutual fund before investing, as they can eat into your overall returns over time.

Like any investment, mutual funds are subject to market risk. The value of the fund's holdings can fluctuate based on the performance of the underlying securities it invests in. If the market experiences a downturn or if the fund's investments perform poorly, the value of your investment can decrease.

Exchange-Traded Funds (ETFs)

ETFs are investment funds that are similar to mutual funds in terms of providing diversification through a collection of securities. However, ETFs are traded on stock exchanges, just like individual stocks. This means that investors can buy and sell ETF shares throughout the trading day at market prices, whereas mutual funds are typically bought and sold at the end of the trading day at the net asset value (NAV) price.

One of the advantages of ETFs is their intraday liquidity. You have the flexibility to buy or sell ETF shares at any time during market hours, unlike mutual funds where you have to wait until the end of the day. Additionally, ETFs provide transparency of holdings, meaning you can easily see what securities the ETF holds.

ETFs also have lower expense ratios compared to some mutual funds. Expense ratios are the fees charged by the fund for managing the investments. Lower expenses can potentially result in higher returns for investors over time.

Similar to mutual funds, ETFs are also subject to market risk and the performance of the underlying securities. The value of an ETF can fluctuate based on how the individual stocks or bonds held by the fund perform. If the market or specific investments decline in value, the ETF's price can decrease as well.

Hedge Funds

Hedge funds are investment funds that are not available to everyone but are generally limited to wealthy or financially sophisticated individuals. The main goal of hedge funds is to generate profits for their investors using various investment strategies.

Unlike mutual funds or exchange-traded funds (ETFs), hedge funds have more flexibility in their investment approach. They can employ a wide range of strategies to try to make money. For example, they can take both long positions (buying assets they believe will increase in value) and short positions (selling assets they believe will decrease in value). This allows hedge fund managers to potentially profit from both rising and falling markets.

Hedge funds may also use leverage, which means borrowing money to amplify their investment positions. By doing so, they can potentially increase their returns, but it also amplifies the potential losses. Additionally, hedge funds may utilize derivatives, which are financial instruments that derive their value from an underlying asset. These derivatives can be used to hedge against risks or speculate on market movements.

It's important to note that hedge funds typically have high minimum investment requirements, meaning you need a significant amount of money to invest. They also charge performance fees, which are based on the returns they generate for their investors. These fees are usually a percentage of the profits earned by the hedge fund. This fee structure incentivizes the fund manager to generate positive returns, as they only earn fees if they successfully make money for their investors.

However, it's essential to understand that hedge funds come with risks. The strategies they employ can be complex and speculative, and they may experience significant fluctuations in value. Furthermore, because they are not as tightly regulated as other investment vehicles, hedge funds may have less transparency and fewer reporting requirements, which can make it more difficult for investors to fully understand their investments.

In summary, hedge funds are private investment funds that aim to generate profits using various strategies. They are typically available to wealthy individuals and have high minimum investment requirements. Hedge funds can use different investment techniques, such as long and short positions, leverage, and derivatives. While they offer potential for higher returns, they also come with increased risks and may have less transparency compared to other investment options.

Private Equity

Private equity is an investment approach where individuals or groups invest money in companies that are not publicly traded on the stock market. Instead of buying shares in a company like you would with stocks, private equity involves acquiring ownership or stakes in businesses that are privately held.

Private equity firms raise funds from large investors like pension funds, endowments, and wealthy individuals. These funds are then used to invest in companies that show potential for growth and profitability. The goal of private equity is to generate attractive returns on investment over the long term.

One characteristic of private equity investments is the longer investment horizon compared to other investment options. Instead of expecting immediate returns, private equity investors are willing to hold their investments for several years. This longer time frame allows the private equity firms to actively work with the companies they invest in, implementing strategies to improve performance and increase the company's value.

Private equity firms often take an active role in managing the companies they invest in. They may bring in experienced professionals or industry experts to provide guidance and support to the company's management team. This can involve making operational improvements, optimizing business processes, or implementing growth strategies to enhance the company's profitability and market position.

Private equity investments can offer attractive returns, but they also carry certain risks. Investing in privately-held companies can be more complex and less liquid compared to publicly traded stocks. It's important to thoroughly evaluate the investment opportunities, conduct due diligence on the companies, and assess the track record and expertise of the private equity firm managing the investments.

Private equity investments are typically suitable for institutional investors and high-net-worth individuals who can afford to allocate a significant amount of capital for an extended period. It's advisable to seek advice from financial professionals or investment advisors who specialize in private equity to understand the potential risks and rewards associated with this investment strategy.

Venture Capital

Venture capital is a type of investment that focuses on supporting early-stage companies with high growth potential. These are often startups or small businesses that have innovative ideas, unique technologies, or disruptive business models. Venture capital firms provide funding to these companies in exchange for a share of ownership, allowing them to participate in the company's success.

Unlike traditional bank loans or public investments, venture capital is more than just providing money. Venture capitalists, who are professionals working for venture capital firms, also bring their expertise, experience, and network to help these startups grow and succeed. They offer guidance, mentorship, and strategic advice to the entrepreneurs and management teams of the invested companies.

Venture capital investments are considered higher risk because many startups fail to achieve the expected growth or profitability. However, venture capitalists understand this risk and aim to invest in companies with significant growth potential. They carefully evaluate the business model, market opportunity, competitive landscape, and management team before making an investment decision.

The goal of venture capital is to identify startups that have the potential to become successful and highly valued companies in the future. If a venture-backed company succeeds and becomes profitable, the venture capitalists can realize significant returns on their investment. This can be achieved through an initial public offering (IPO), where the company goes public and its shares are traded on the stock market, or through an acquisition by a larger company.

Venture capital investments are not suitable for all investors. They typically require a longer investment horizon and involve higher levels of risk compared to more traditional investments. Venture capital firms often have specific investment criteria and focus on particular industries or sectors.

For entrepreneurs and founders of startups, venture capital can be a valuable source of funding and support to bring their innovative ideas to life and scale their businesses.

However, it's important for both entrepreneurs and investors to carefully consider the potential risks and rewards associated with venture capital investments and seek advice from professionals with expertise in this field.

Retirement Accounts: Contributing to retirement accounts, such as 401(k)s or individual retirement accounts (IRAs), can provide tax advantages and long-term wealth accumulation. These accounts often offer a variety of investment options, including stocks, bonds, and mutual funds, and may provide tax-deferred or tax-free growth.

Business Ownership and Entrepreneurship: Starting your own business or investing in existing businesses can be a way to generate wealth. This avenue comes with risks and requires careful planning, market analysis, and management skills. However, successful businesses can provide significant returns and wealth creation opportunities.

Commodities and Precious Metals: Investing in commodities like gold, silver, oil, or agricultural products can be another way to diversify your portfolio. These investments can serve as a hedge against inflation or economic uncertainty. However, it's important to understand the specific dynamics and risks associated with commodity markets.

Peer-to-Peer Lending: Peer-to-peer lending platforms connect borrowers with individual lenders, cutting out traditional financial institutions. By lending money to individuals or small businesses, investors can earn interest on their loans. This investment option requires careful evaluation of borrowers' creditworthiness and an understanding of the associated risks.

Cryptocurrencies: Cryptocurrencies, such as Bitcoin or Ethereum, have gained popularity as an alternative investment. These digital assets operate on decentralized networks and offer the potential for high returns. However, they also come with volatility and regulatory risks, so it's essential to conduct thorough research and exercise caution when investing in cryptocurrencies.

Private equity, venture capital, hedge funds, commodities, precious metals, or cryptocurrencies are non-traditional asset classes that offer diversification and potentially higher returns.. They often have different risk and return profiles compared to traditional asset classes, and they can provide opportunities for capital appreciation and portfolio differentiation.

Have a Balanced Investment Approach

A balanced investment approach involves allocating your portfolio across various asset classes to achieve a mix of growth and stability. Here are some key benefits of a balanced investment approach:

Risk Mitigation: Diversifying your portfolio across different asset classes helps reduce the overall risk. When one asset class underperforms, others may provide stability or better returns, offsetting potential losses.

Capital Preservation: Including conservative assets, such as bonds or cash equivalents, in your portfolio helps preserve capital during market downturns. These assets act as a cushion and can provide stability when other riskier investments experience volatility.

Growth Potential: Allocating a portion of your portfolio to growth-oriented assets, such as stocks or alternative investments, allows you to participate in the potential for higher returns. These assets have the potential to outperform over the long term and contribute to the growth of your portfolio.

Income Generation: Investing in income-generating assets, such as dividend-paying stocks or bonds, can provide a steady stream of income. This income can be reinvested or used to cover living expenses, enhancing your overall financial well-being.

Flexibility and Adaptability: A balanced investment approach provides flexibility to adapt to changing market conditions. It allows you to adjust your asset allocation based on your risk tolerance, investment goals, and market outlook. This adaptability helps in optimizing your portfolio's performance over time.

POINTS TO NOTE

a. Asset Allocation: Asset allocation refers to the distribution of your investments across different asset classes. It involves determining the optimal mix of stocks, bonds, real estate, and other asset classes based on your financial goals, risk tolerance, and time horizon. Asset allocation aims to balance risk and return by diversifying across various investments.

b. Risk Management: Effective risk management involves understanding and managing the risks associated with each investment. This includes analyzing factors such as market risk, credit risk, liquidity risk, and geopolitical risk. Risk management strategies may include diversification, setting risk limits, regular portfolio reviews, and implementing risk mitigation techniques.

c. Rebalancing: Regularly rebalancing your portfolio is crucial to maintaining the desired asset allocation. Rebalancing involves adjusting the allocation of your investments to bring it back in line with your target allocation. This process ensures that your portfolio stays aligned with your investment goals and risk tolerance.

It is important to note that asset allocation and risk management should be personalized based on individual circumstances, goals, and risk tolerance. Consulting with a financial advisor or investment professional can help you develop an appropriate asset allocation strategy and manage risk effectively. Now, let's get back to Oliver's story.

Chapter 12

ESTATE PLANNING AND WEALTH PRESERVATION

Oliver's time on Earth drew to a close, but his spirit lived on in the hearts of those who continued the work he had started. His story would be passed down through generations, inspiring countless others to embark on their own journeys of investing and philanthropy.

As Oliver took his final breath, he knew that his life had been extraordinary. The rich boy who once yearned for purpose had found it in the pursuit of creating extraordinary wealth, not just for himself but for the betterment of humanity.

And so, the story of Oliver Blackwood's guide to investing became a timeless tale of ambition, compassion, and the transformative power of wealth. It reminded the world that with knowledge, foresight, and a commitment to making a difference, everyday people could rise above their circumstances and create extraordinary wealth that would shape the world for generations to come.

Estate planning is a crucial component of financial management that ensures the smooth transfer of wealth to future generations while preserving your assets and minimizing tax liabilities. It is not just about distributing assets after death but also about preserving wealth and ensuring that it is transferred according to your wishes.

Here are key reasons why estate planning is important for wealth preservation:

Control and Distribution of Assets: Estate planning allows you to have control over how your assets will be distributed among your heirs and beneficiaries. It ensures that your wishes are carried out and prevents disputes or conflicts among family members.

Minimization of Taxes and Expenses: Through strategic estate planning, you can minimize estate taxes and other expenses that could erode the value of your estate. Proper planning can help maximize the amount passed on to your beneficiaries.

Asset Protection: Estate planning can help protect your assets from potential creditors, lawsuits, or other financial risks. By utilizing legal structures and trusts, you can safeguard your wealth for the benefit of your intended beneficiaries.

Continuity of Business or Charitable Endeavors: If you own a business or have philanthropic goals, estate planning allows for the seamless continuation of these endeavors after your passing. It ensures that your business is managed or your charitable objectives are upheld according to your wishes.

Estate Planning Tools

Estate planning tools are legal instruments or strategies that help you ensure that your assets are distributed according to your wishes after you pass away. These tools are designed to protect and manage assets, minimize taxes, and provide for the smooth transfer of wealth to beneficiaries. Here are some commonly used estate planning tools:

Will: A will is a legal document that outlines how a person's assets will be distributed after their death. It allows individuals to specify who will receive their property, appoint guardians for minor children, and name an executor to oversee the distribution of assets.

Trust: A trust is a legal entity that holds assets for the benefit of beneficiaries. There are different types of trusts, such as revocable living trusts and irrevocable trusts. Trusts can help avoid probate, provide for ongoing management of assets, and maintain privacy. They can also offer tax planning benefits and protect assets from creditors.

Power of Attorney: A power of attorney is a document that designates someone to make financial or medical decisions on your behalf if you become incapacitated. It allows a trusted person, known as an agent or attorney-in-fact, to manage your affairs and make decisions according to your wishes.

Advance Healthcare Directive/Living Will: These documents outline your healthcare preferences and end-of-life treatment decisions. They specify your desires regarding life-sustaining treatments, organ donation, and appoint a healthcare proxy to make medical decisions on your behalf if you are unable to do so.

Beneficiary Designations: Beneficiary designations are used for assets such as life insurance policies, retirement accounts, and payable-on-death bank accounts. By naming beneficiaries, you can ensure that these assets pass directly to the designated individuals, bypassing the probate process.

Life Insurance: Life insurance can be an essential estate planning tool. It provides a death benefit to your beneficiaries upon your passing, which can help replace lost income, cover debts, or pay for final expenses. Life insurance proceeds are generally tax-free for the beneficiaries.

Family Limited Partnership (FLP) or Family Limited Liability Company (LLC): These entities can be used for estate planning purposes, particularly for high-net-worth individuals. They allow for the centralized management of family assets, facilitate intergenerational wealth transfer, and offer potential tax benefits.

Charitable Trusts: Charitable trusts allow individuals to support charitable causes while also providing potential tax advantages. These trusts enable the transfer of assets to a charitable organization while providing income to the donor or other beneficiaries during their lifetime.

Your estate planning tools should be tailored to your circumstances and goals. Consulting with an experienced estate planning attorney or financial advisor can help you understand the options available and create a comprehensive plan that aligns with your wishes and objectives.

You can minimize the taxes paid on your assets and ensure smooth wealth transfer when you leverage any of these options:

a. Lifetime Gifting: One strategy to minimize estate taxes is through lifetime gifting. By transferring assets during your lifetime, you can reduce the size of your taxable estate while potentially benefiting from gift tax exemptions or exclusions. Strategic gifting can help you pass wealth to your heirs while reducing potential tax burdens.

b. Trusts for Tax Planning: Various trusts, such as irrevocable life insurance trusts (ILITs) or charitable remainder trusts (CRTs), can be utilized to minimize estate taxes. These trusts provide tax advantages and allow for the efficient transfer of assets to beneficiaries or charitable organizations.

c. Business Succession Planning: If you own a business, implementing a well-structured business succession plan is essential for a smooth transfer of ownership. This involves identifying successors, establishing ownership transition plans, and considering tax-efficient strategies for transferring business assets.

Philanthropy and Charitable Giving

Philanthropy and charitable giving are about giving back and making a positive impact on the causes and organizations that you care about. In estate planning, you have the opportunity to incorporate philanthropy into your plan, and here's how it works:

Charitable Gifts: You can include specific charitable gifts in your estate plan. This means you can designate certain assets or a portion of your estate to be given to charitable organizations upon your passing. These organizations could be nonprofits, educational institutions, medical research centers, or any other cause that you feel strongly about.

Charitable Trusts: Another way to incorporate philanthropy into your estate plan is by creating charitable trusts. These are special legal arrangements where you can place assets or funds into a trust, and the income generated from those assets is used for charitable purposes during your lifetime or after your passing. Charitable trusts provide ongoing support to charitable organizations and can also offer potential tax benefits.

Tax Benefits: One advantage of incorporating philanthropy into your estate plan is the potential for tax benefits. When you make charitable gifts or create charitable trusts, you may be eligible for tax deductions. This means that the value of your charitable contributions can reduce the amount of estate taxes that your estate would otherwise owe. By strategically planning your charitable giving, you can potentially minimize your tax liabilities while supporting causes that are meaningful to you.

Family Involvement: Philanthropy and charitable giving can be a way to involve your family in the estate planning process and pass on your values. You can engage your loved ones in discussions about the causes you support, the impact you want to make, and even involve them in charitable activities while you're alive. This not only creates a sense of shared purpose and family unity, but it also helps instill a spirit of giving back in future generations.

Overall, incorporating philanthropy and charitable giving into your estate plan allows you to leave a lasting legacy and support causes that are important to you. It can provide potential tax benefits, involve your family in the process, and make a positive impact on the world even after you're gone.

Consulting with professionals can help you navigate the specifics of charitable giving and ensure that your philanthropic goals align with your overall estate planning objectives.

Estate planning in general can be complex, involving legal, financial, and tax considerations. It is advisable to work with professional advisors who specialize in estate planning to ensure that your plan is comprehensive, legally sound, and aligned with your goals. Here are some professionals you may consider involving:

a. Estate Planning Attorney: An estate planning attorney will assist you in drafting legal documents, such as wills, trusts, and powers of attorney, that accurately reflect your intentions. They have expertise in estate planning laws and can ensure your plan complies with applicable regulations.

b. Financial Planner: A financial planner can provide guidance on asset management, investment strategies, and overall financial planning. They can help you align your estate planning goals with your broader financial objectives and ensure that your estate plan is integrated into your overall financial strategy.

c. Tax Advisor: A tax advisor, such as a certified public accountant (CPA), can provide valuable insights on tax implications related to your estate plan. They can help you navigate complex tax laws, minimize tax liabilities, and ensure compliance with tax regulations.

d. Trustee or Executor: Consider appointing a trustee or executor who will oversee the administration of your estate and ensure that your wishes are carried out. This individual should be trustworthy, knowledgeable, and capable of managing the legal and financial aspects of your estate.

e. Philanthropic Advisor: If philanthropy and charitable giving are important to you, a philanthropic advisor can help you develop a charitable giving plan that aligns with your values and maximizes the impact of your donations.

Collaborating with these professionals will help you develop a comprehensive estate plan that addresses legal, financial, and tax considerations while aligning with your personal goals and values.

In summary, Estate Planning helps to protect your wealth, establish a legacy, and provide for the financial well-being of your loved ones.

Chapter 13

CULTIVATING A WEALTHY MINDSET

Investing can be a challenging journey that requires not only financial knowledge and skills but also the right mindset and psychological resilience. In this section, we will discuss common challenges and roadblocks in investing, strategies to overcome fear, doubt, and other psychological barriers to success, the mindset and habits of successful investors, and provide tools and techniques to cultivate a wealthy mindset for long-term financial success.

Common Challenges and Roadblocks in Investing

a. Fear and Emotions: Investing often involves uncertainty, market volatility, and the risk of financial loss. Fear and emotions, such as anxiety or greed, can cloud judgment and lead to irrational investment decisions.

b. Lack of Knowledge: Investing requires a certain level of financial literacy and understanding of investment concepts. Lack of knowledge can lead to confusion, poor decision-making, and missed opportunities.

c.   Short-Term Thinking: Many investors focus on short-term gains and react impulsively to market fluctuations. This can hinder their ability to see the bigger picture and make sound long-term investment decisions.

d.   Overconfidence and Bias: Overconfidence can lead investors to underestimate risks or overestimate their abilities, leading to excessive risk-taking. Cognitive biases, such as confirmation bias or herd mentality, can also impact investment decisions.

Strategies to Overcome Psychological Barriers

a.   Education and Knowledge: Investing in your financial education is crucial. Continuously learn about investment strategies, asset classes, and risk management techniques. This knowledge will empower you to make informed decisions and mitigate emotional reactions.

b. Goal Setting and Planning: Set clear investment goals and develop a well-defined investment plan. Having a structured approach can help you stay focused and make rational decisions, even in times of market volatility.

c. Risk Management and Diversification: Implement risk management strategies, such as diversifying your portfolio across different asset classes and maintaining an appropriate asset allocation. This can help reduce the impact of individual investments and manage risk effectively.

d. Emotional Discipline: Practice emotional discipline by maintaining a long-term perspective and avoiding impulsive reactions to short-term market fluctuations. Emotions should not drive investment decisions, but rather be based on rational analysis and your investment plan.

Mindset and Habits of Successful Investors

a. Patience and Long-Term Orientation: Successful investors understand the value of patience and adopt a long-term mindset. They focus on the big picture and are not swayed by short-term market movements.

b. Continuous Learning: Successful investors are lifelong learners. They stay informed about market trends, economic indicators, and new investment opportunities. They actively seek knowledge and adapt their strategies accordingly.

c. Discipline and Consistency: Consistency is key to successful investing. Successful investors stick to their investment plan, avoid impulsive decisions, and maintain discipline in their investment approach.

d. Risk Management: Successful investors understand the importance of managing risk. They diversify their portfolios, set risk limits, and regularly review and adjust their investments to align with their risk tolerance and goals.

Cultivating a Wealthy Mindset

a. Positive Thinking: Cultivate a positive mindset and believe in your ability to achieve financial success. Surround yourself with positive influences and affirmations that reinforce your financial goals and aspirations.

b. Visualization and Goal Setting: Visualize your financial goals and regularly review them to stay motivated. Set specific, measurable, achievable, relevant, and time-bound (SMART) goals that align with your vision of wealth.

c. Continuous Self-Improvement: Invest in personal development and self-improvement to enhance your financial knowledge, skills, and mindset. Read books, attend seminars, listen to podcasts, and surround yourself with like-minded individuals who inspire and motivate you.

d. Persistence and Resilience: Building wealth through investing requires persistence and resilience. There will be ups and downs in the market, and setbacks are inevitable. Successful investors stay committed to their long-term goals, learn from failures, and bounce back from challenges.

e. Mindfulness and Emotional Intelligence: Practice mindfulness to stay present and focused on your investment decisions. Develop emotional intelligence to understand and manage your emotions effectively, particularly during times of market volatility or financial stress.

f. Networking and Mentorship: Surround yourself with a supportive network of investors and seek mentorship from experienced individuals in the field. Learn from their experiences, seek advice, and leverage their wisdom to enhance your own investment journey.

g. Gratitude and Giving Back: Cultivate a sense of gratitude for the wealth you have already accumulated and the opportunities you have. Giving back to society through philanthropy or charitable endeavors can provide a sense of fulfillment and purpose, enhancing your overall mindset towards wealth.

Tools and Techniques to Cultivate a Wealthy Mindset

a. Visualization and Affirmations: Practice visualization techniques where you vividly imagine achieving your financial goals. Use positive affirmations related to wealth and abundance to reprogram your subconscious mind for success.

b. Journaling and Reflection: Maintain a journal to record your investment decisions, emotions, and reflections. Regularly review and reflect on your experiences to learn from your successes and failures, identify patterns, and make adjustments to your mindset and strategies.

c. Meditation and Mindfulness Practices: Incorporate meditation and mindfulness practices into your daily routine to cultivate clarity, focus, and emotional balance. These practices can help you develop a calm and centered mindset that is less susceptible to market fluctuations.

d. Positive Role Models and Inspirational Content: Seek inspiration from successful investors and financial experts through books, podcasts, videos, or seminars. Engage with content that promotes a wealthy mindset and provides insights into successful investment strategies.

e. Continuous Education: Stay updated with the latest trends and developments in the investment world through ongoing education. Attend workshops, webinars, or conferences, enroll in investment courses, and leverage online resources to expand your knowledge and stay ahead of the curve.

Remember that investing is not just about financial strategies but also about personal growth and developing the mindset necessary for long-term success.

Chapter 14

BUILDING A NETWORK AND LEVERAGING EXPERTISE

Building a strong network and leveraging the expertise of others is crucial for success in any endeavor, including investing. In this section, we will highlight the importance of building a network of like-minded individuals and industry experts, discuss ways to find mentors and advisors, explore resources for ongoing education, and discuss the benefits of joining investment clubs, attending conferences, and participating in online communities.

Importance of Building a Network

a. Knowledge and Insights: Building a network allows you to tap into the knowledge and insights of others who have experience in investing. By connecting with like-minded individuals and industry experts, you gain access to valuable information, different perspectives, and insights into investment strategies and opportunities.

b. Support and Guidance: A strong network provides a support system that can offer guidance, advice, and emotional support during your investment journey. Surrounding yourself with individuals who share your goals and aspirations can motivate you and provide encouragement when facing challenges.

c. Collaborative Opportunities: Networking opens doors to collaborative opportunities such as joint ventures, partnerships, and co-investing. Through your network, you may find potential investment partners, access deal flow, and share resources, expanding your investment opportunities.

Finding Mentors and Advisors

a. Identify Potential Mentors: Look for successful investors or professionals in the investment field who align with your investment goals and values. Consider individuals who have achieved the level of success you aspire to and possess the expertise you seek.

b. Reach out and Establish Relationships: Reach out to potential mentors or advisors through professional networks, industry events, or introductions from mutual connections. Initiate conversations, express your interest in learning from their experience, and demonstrate your commitment and willingness to grow.

c. Participate in Mentorship Programs: Some organizations or communities offer formal mentorship programs that connect experienced investors with individuals seeking guidance. Look for such programs within investment clubs, professional associations, or educational institutions.

Resources for Ongoing Education

a. Books and Publications: Invest in educational books, magazines, and publications focused on investment strategies, financial markets, and economic trends. These resources provide in-depth knowledge and insights from renowned authors and experts in the field.

b. Online Courses and Webinars: Enroll in online investment courses and webinars to enhance your knowledge and skills. These courses are designed to provide structured learning, covering various aspects of investing, including fundamental analysis, technical analysis, risk management, and portfolio construction.

c. Financial News and Market Analysis: Stay updated with financial news and market analysis through reputable sources. Follow news outlets, financial publications, and websites that provide comprehensive coverage of the financial markets. This will help you stay informed about market trends, economic indicators, and potential investment opportunities.

d. Professional Associations and Conferences: Joining professional associations related to finance and investing provides access to educational resources, industry events, and networking opportunities. Attend conferences and seminars where you can learn from experts, participate in panel discussions, and engage in valuable networking.

e. Investment Clubs and Meetups: Join local investment clubs or attend meetups where individuals with similar interests gather to discuss investment strategies, share experiences, and learn from one another. These forums provide a supportive environment for networking and knowledge exchange.

f. Social Media Groups: Participate in social media groups or forums focused on investing, where you can connect with individuals who share your interests. Engage in discussions, ask questions, and learn from the experiences and insights of other members.

By staying connected with professionals in the field and staying informed about market trends, you can enhance your investment knowledge, expand your network, and improve your overall investment decision-making capabilities.

Chapter 15

CASE STUDIES:
REAL-LIFE EXAMPLES OF EXTRAORDINARY WEALTH CREATION

Let us examine real-life success stories of individuals who have achieved extraordinary wealth through investing. We will explore some notable case studies of successful investors, examining their strategies, challenges faced, and key lessons learned.

Warren Buffett

Warren Buffett is one of the most renowned and successful investors in history. His approach to value investing and long-term wealth creation has made him a billionaire. Buffett emphasizes the importance of thorough research, investing in businesses with a durable competitive advantage, and holding investments for the long term. His journey demonstrates the power of patience, disciplined investing, and taking a contrarian approach.

Key Lessons From Warren Buffet

Focus on intrinsic value: Buffett emphasizes the importance of understanding the intrinsic value of an investment and buying at a discount to that value.

Long-term perspective: He advocates for a long-term investment horizon and avoiding short-term market fluctuations.

Diversification within expertise: Buffett suggests focusing on areas where you have expertise and diversifying within that scope.

Learning from mistakes: Buffett acknowledges that mistakes are inevitable, but learning from them and adapting is crucial for long-term success.

Peter Lynch

Peter Lynch is known for his successful tenure as the manager of the Fidelity Magellan Fund, where he achieved remarkable returns. Lynch's investment philosophy focused on investing in companies that he understood, had a competitive advantage, and had the potential for growth. He coined the term "invest in what you know" and emphasized the importance of thorough research and understanding the businesses you invest in.

Key Lessons From Peter Lynch

Be patient and disciplined: Lynch advises investors to be patient, as successful investments often take time to materialize. It's essential to stay disciplined and not be swayed by short-term market fluctuations.

Invest in familiar industries: Lynch suggests investing in industries or companies that you understand and have knowledge about.

Analyze growth potential: Lynch looks for companies with the potential for long-term growth and sustainable competitive advantages.

Stay informed: He emphasizes the importance of staying informed about the companies you invest in and tracking industry trends.

John Templeton

John Templeton was a legendary investor who used a global value investing approach to build substantial wealth.

He believed in buying stocks that were undervalued and had the potential for future growth. Templeton also emphasized the importance of maintaining a contrarian approach and taking advantage of market pessimism.

Key Lessons From John Templeton

Contrarian investing: Templeton advises investors to be contrarian and invest when others are fearful, as it presents opportunities to buy undervalued assets.

Diversify globally: He advocated for global diversification, emphasizing that opportunities for growth exist beyond domestic markets.

Patience and long-term perspective: Templeton believed in the power of compounding returns over the long term, highlighting the importance of patience and a long-term investment horizon.

Value investing: He emphasized the value investing approach, focusing on buying assets at a discount to their intrinsic value.

These case studies provide insights into the strategies, challenges, and lessons learned by successful investors.

Some common themes that emerge include the importance of thorough research, disciplined investing, a long-term perspective, and being open to learning from mistakes. It is crucial to adapt these strategies to individual circumstances and investment goals.

By studying the experiences of successful investors, you will gain inspiration and practical knowledge to apply to your own investment journeys. However, it's important to remember that each investor's path is unique, and it is essential to develop a personalized investment strategy based on individual risk tolerance, financial goals, and time horizon.

I hope you got value from this book.